National Politics Is Everybody's Business

John D. Rigazio

authorHOUSE®

AuthorHouse™
1663 Liberty Drive, Suite 200
Bloomington, IN 47403
www.authorhouse.com
Phone: 1-800-839-8640

First published by AuthorHouse 7/2/2008

ISBN: 978-1-4343-9344-9 (sc)
ISBN: 978-1-4343-9345-6 (hc)

Library of Congress Control Number: 2008905452

Printed in the United States of America
Bloomington, Indiana

This book is printed on acid-free paper.

www.JohnRigazio.com

DEDICATION

This book is dedicated to Kelly McKenna, without whom I couldn't have put my memoirs into book form; also to my fiancée of eight years, Theresa Marie Franke, who kept me alive while dealing with my diabetes and depression; and to all of the local readers of my political column, National Politics is Everybody's Business.

Thank you,

John Donald Rigazio

CONTENTS

PREFACE

I, John Donald Rigazio, ran for President of the United States in the 2004 NH primaries against President Bush and 13 others.

I have listed my interviews, ads, and political positions on the War in Iraq and the false economy. You will see the foresight I had in 2004, and that many of the same problems are still with us.

I am sorry the book has little order and some chapters should be rewritten. However, that being said, please buy and read this book. I have been writing a column (*National Politics is Everybody's Business*) for five years now and have a large following in the local newspapers.

One thing is for sure, the Republicans, Democrats, so called Liberals, and so called Conservatives will all have to become Nationalists if we want to go back to the America we once knew.

INTRODUCTION

If America is going to maintain our national sovereignty and control our own economic destiny, we must recognize the path which globalization is leading us on. If allowed to continue, UNFAIR world trade will lower the standard of living for the majority of us Americans.

As more and more Americans cannot provide for themselves, other hard-working taxpayers will be forced to pay much higher taxes at the city, state and federal level, thus changing our democracy to a socialistic government. While we didn't vote for socialism at the ballot box, that's what we are going to get because of our fiscal irresponsibility.

If we go one step further, socialism enforced by state and federal government troops is communism, isn't it?

When the next president is sworn in in January 2009, America will be in a full blown recession/depression. Why I state recession and depression is that many Americans will be in this recession period; however, more and more Americans who cannot put food on the table, pay their rent or mortgage, put gas in their gas tank, pay their oil heating bills, and pay their ever increasing city, state and federal taxes will be in a depression.

The old saying is it's a recession when your NEIGHBOR is out of work, but it's a depression when YOU are out of work. As the recession pushes more and more of us Americans into a depression, the recession will last years and the violence in America's cities will escalate.

There are many things America must do as soon as possible. The first is to look out for the best interests of America first, and the world second. Then we must bring the trade deficit down to zero or as near zero as possible. The American economy cannot continue providing the world economy with good paying jobs at our expense.

Let me see now; they tell us a weak dollar made our exports cheaper all over the world market and world products higher on the American market. I see a weak dollar for years to come, so why can't we get a zero balance on trade? We in America must stop our deficit spending, balance our federal budget, and start paying down on our national debt; we must push for a zero trade deficit. Our present American economy is unsustainable.

The American people will soon realize that George W. Bush not only handled the Iraq War wrong from beginning to end but his policy of "deficits don't matter" has bankrupted the country.

With Hillary, Obama and McCain to choose from, I hereby am declaring my vote for Hillary. God bless her, and God bless America. If Obama is the Democratic nominee for president, I will support him.

1

PUBLISHED JAN. 3, 2008

1964: THE YEAR I LOST MY MARBLES

I never went to college and I am computer illiterate. So what is it in my education that gives me the right to offer constructive criticism to our federal government on the many grave problems facing our country?

Over and above my constitutional right of freedom of speech, I hereby give you my educational background.

The first part of my education was strong parental guidance; secondly, I was drafted and spent two years (November 1952 to November 1954) in the U.S. Army Infantry, which was an education in itself. I was a businessman for 50 years in the wholesale/retail food business, dealing with the biggest business in the U.S. I watch all the TV news and financial channels, and I read one or more newspapers every day.

Perhaps my greatest education on what it means to be an American came from a great American (my father), John Batista Rigazio, who passed away in 1949. I was 17 and had just graduated from Spaulding High.

My father was the only person in his family who came over from Italy as a teenager. He was 58 when he died. He worked in the brickyards and later opened three retail fruit and produce businesses, plus one wholesale produce route. He himself spoke three languages fluently; however, he would not allow my mother to teach us Italian.

In his mind, we were Americans of Italian descent, not Italians living in America. He ingrained many American values in me which are too many to list. However, the one I could never forget was America was the land of opportunity, not the land of guarantee.

So in 1964, I was a 33-year-old businessman and family man and never wrote a letter to the editor, never questioned my federal government's decisions. However, that all changed when Lyndon Baines Johnson (LBJ) gave his inaugural speech. He said, in essence, America was a nation of unprecedented wealth. He listed many of our great assets.

He then said amongst all this wealth we in America still had citizens living in poverty, citizens not being able to afford a college education, some not having adequate health care, and last but not least, our older citizens were in need of federal programs to take care of them.

What LBJ said in his 1964 inaugural speech was he was GUARANTEEING all Americans everything because they were Americans.

My father, John Batista Rigazio (JBR), told me America was the land of OPPORTUNITY, not the land of guarantee.

From 1964 (the year I lost my marbles) I have been following our country's building on the 1964/68 socialistic foundation laid out by LBJ and his Great Society programs.

There is no way in a letter to the editor I could give readers my views of America's 1964 march to socialism. I will say, however, that we have more people dependent upon government to maintain their living standards. This is a direct result of trying to change America from the land of opportunity to the land of guarantee.

I suppose in retrospect if America could socialize on a balanced budget it would be OK. However, as President Reagan said, "A government big enough to give you everything you want is big enough to take everything you've got."

Note: LBJ, from 1964-68, passed 450 socialistic bills, laying down the foundation for socialistic growth in America. I feel about 150 bills were probably needed and many existing laws needed to be enforced.

He meant well; however, my father (JBR) knew you cannot change America from the land of opportunity to the land of guarantee.

2

PUBLISHED JULY 26, 2007

THERE ARE NO MIDDLE CLASS AMERICANS

For years now the media has been telling us Americans we are either poor, middle class or rich. First of all, there is no class system in America. Any American citizen can be born poor and still become rich. Second, if the media insists on segregating us Americans according to our incomes, let's do it right.

Yes, the poor can be put into one group and the rich can be put into another group. But the rest of us Americans CANNOT be put into one group called the middle class. Under this false terminology, a family making $20,000 a year and a family making $500,000 a year could fall under America's middle class. Get the picture? This is too much of a discrepancy in incomes to call all of us MIDDLE CLASS. So, if the media wants to separate us Americans according to our incomes, let's do it right.

First of all, we have the POOR families who make $10,000 to $20,000 a year; then we have the LOWER INCOME families who make $20,000 to $40,000 a year; then we have the MIDDLE INCOME families making $40,000 to $100,000 a year; then we have the HIGHER INCOME families making $100,000 to $500,000 a year; and then there are the RICH FAMILIES who can live on their interest for the rest of their lives, and their children and grandchildren will be born wealthy.

One of the things that always bothered me about classifying all of us Americans as middle class was that the media called some of us HIGHER MIDDLE CLASS, so some of us have to be called LOWER MIDDLE CLASS.

Take it from me, I have seen many so-called UPPER middle class who have NO CLASS at all, and I have seen so-called LOWER middle class work two jobs, accept no government programs and bring up their families to obey the laws of the land. THESE LOWER CLASS FAMILIES HAVE CLASS.

So what we have to do in America is provide the POOR with the opportunity to provide for themselves and their family, and for the LOWER INCOME families to remain self-sufficient and try to climb the ladder to middle income status, and for the MIDDLE INCOME families to maintain their status and strive to become HIGHER INCOME families, and for the higher

3

income to maintain their higher living standards, which pay the most taxes and purchase the most goods and services. For the rich, I say take that tax cut and invest in America to create jobs. Investing in foreign countries may increase your bottom line, but you will be like the winners of a poker game on the Titanic.

By the way, the Titanic is America and the iceberg is right on course with our economy.

No, the rich are not getting any richer and the poor are not getting any poorer; however, the LOWER INCOME, MIDDLE INCOME and HIGHER INCOME American families are working two and three jobs just to maintain their standard of living. By the way, they are fighting a losing battle as more and more Americans are going down the economic ladder instead of going up the economic ladder. We must REVERSE this trend.

In this commentary I use the term "family incomes" as we all know it takes two paychecks for the majority of Americans to maintain our standards of living. Also, the suggested incomes in the columns are gross amounts, not take-home pay. So there is no middle class; however, we still can call our paycheck TAKE HOME PAY for after Uncle Sam takes out the taxes the only place you can go with your pay is home.

3

CHINA'S MOST FAVORED NATION STATUS MUST END NOW

Most-favored-nation (MFN) status offers low tariffs and treats countries as normal trading partners.

Termination of China's MFN status would result in duty increases on about 95 percent of U.S. imports from China. The cost effect of the increases would vary among the various product groups, but would on the whole be substantial.

In view of the overall substantial differences between the concessional (MFN) and full rates of duty, it is clear that the termination of China's MFN status would result in substantial increases in the cost of imports from China. Based on our survey of the 87 individual items whose imports in 1995 exceeded $100 million each and whose total accounted for $23.2 million (51 percent) of all U.S. imports from China in that year, the termination of China's MFN status would increase the average importers' cost of Chinese products by some 35 percent, in most individual instances between 25 and 65 percent.

Despite a strained relationship after China's 1989 crackdown of protestors in Tiananmen Square, China has been granted a MFN waiver every year since 1980.

THE MAIN REASON WHY THE U.S. MUST WITHDRAW CHINA'S MOST FAVORED NATION STATUS

No, it is not their human rights records, or their unfair trade practices, or unfair manipulation of their currency to increase their exports to America while extracting cash from our economy.

CHINA MUST GO because they sold Pakistan the nuclear supplies it needed to have atomic weapons.

We pay Pakistan $12 billion a year to fight off the terrorists in Southern Pakistan; however, the $12 billion is not being used for that.

Osama Bin Laden and Al Qaeda have a sanctuary in Southern Pakistan where they terrorize Afghanistan and America cannot go into Pakistan to bomb them or disrupt their training.

Why is this? The Pakistani government will not let America go after the terrorists in Southern Pakistan because Pakistan has nuclear weapons supplied to them by China.

This is the main reason the U.S. must not resume its MFN status with China next year.

Will this action bring on a trade war with China? Probably yes; however, better sooner than later – they need us as much as we need them. It's the price we have to pay to maintain our national sovereignty and to control our own economic destiny.

4

PUBLISHED IN THE ROCHESTER COURIER, 1950

PERTINENT PERSONALITIES: MY MOTHER

Pen sketches of women in this part of New England who have contributed to its moral, industrial, social or spiritual growth

When the Golden Rule Foundation was casting about for candidates for "The Mother of the Year," they overlooked one very imminent possibility in the person of Lena Rigazio, mother of three and a woman to whom the American ideal of democracy is a never-ending source of wonder and delight.

BORN IN ITALY

Born in the lovely old medieval town of Cigliano in Northern Italy, Mrs. Rigazio came to the United States as a girl of six years and settled with her family in Haverhill, Mass. She attended the Haverhill schools, and when she had completed her formal education was employed as a sample stitcher in one of the great shoe manufacturing plants there.

During her years in Haverhill she met John Rigazio, who was just starting a fruit business in Rochester, and they were married on Sept. 18, 1926. They took an apartment owned by the late Lena Morrison on Summer Street and Mrs. Rigazio remembers that Mrs. Morrison gave her an acquaintance party in which all the neighbors took part. Among the guests were Mrs. Dorothy Lyons, wife of the present Mayor C. Wesley Lyons, and her sister, Mrs. Marion Ross, and she has always been grateful for their friendliness and aid in making acquaintances.

BUILT LARGE BUSINESS

Both Mr. and Mrs. Rigazio became naturalized American citizens as soon as possible after settling in Rochester and together they built a wholesale and retail fruit business that today covers a wide area in southeastern New Hampshire. John, a cheerful, honest man, made friends readily and held them. Mrs. Rigazio did the bookkeeping for the business and between times raised three fine children. The two sons, Raymond and

7

John, both graduated from Spaulding High School and the daughter, June, is a junior at Holy Rosary High.

Raymond, or "Butch" as he is known, was a football ace at Spaulding and on the death of his father last year took over the management of the business with the assistance of his mother. John is associated with them in the enterprise.

The thing that most of Mrs. Rigazio's friends will remember about her probably will be her eyes and her smile. Her lovely brown eyes reflect the kindliness of a great soul and her smile has made her the friend of hundreds of people. A deeply religious woman, she has always found comfort in her church and the peace she has found there has been reflected so many times in the cheerfulness with which she greets everyone.

LOVES AMERICA

Mrs. Rigazio has known many sorrows, but the deep goodness that is inherent in her disposition has made her known and loved by all with whom she has made friends. And through all the years since she first came to these shores, she has never ceased to wonder at the opportunities which are available to any person who is willing to work hard, honor their God and their fellow men.

5

PUBLISHED NOV. 6, 2003 IN THE ROCHESTER TIMES
Reprinted courtesy of John Nolan and *The Rochester Times*

RIGAZIO SIGNS UP
FOR PRESIDENTIAL PRIMARY

By JOHN NOLAN

ROCHESTER – Rochester businessman John Rigazio was third in line to pay the $1,000 fee for the first-in-the-nation primary, and declare himself a candidate for the Presidency of the United States of America, on the morning of Monday, Nov. 3.

Rigazio said he arrived at the New Hampshire Secretary of State's office in Concord a few minutes before 8 a.m. and found himself behind another Republican candidate, Robert Haines of Manchester, who had apparently camped out overnight. Second in line was a Democratic candidate, Harry Braun of Phoenix, Ariz., whose main electoral plank is making America energy independent with a hydrogen production system.

With members of the national media in attendance, Rigazio said he spoke for about 15 minutes (after signing up) on the importance of winning the war in Iraq and the need to get out of the World Trade Organization.

After several months of campaigning as a Democrat, Rigazio recently registered as a Republican, concluding that he would attract more support by doing so.

6

PUBLISHED IN 2003 IN THE ROCHESTER TIMES
Reprinted courtesy of John Nolan and *The Rochester Times*

AND NOW THERE'S 10 (OR 11)

Rochester businessman to spend $100G of own cash in NH presidential primary

By JOHN NOLAN

ROCHESTER – John Rigazio, businessman, political commentator and Rochester native, formally declared his candidacy for the presidency of the United States last week, and immediately demanded equal billing with nine nationally-known candidates who have already stated their intentions to be on the ballot for the first-in-the-nation Democratic primary in New Hampshire, early in 2004.

(Actually, there are *already* 10 nationally known candidates trysting for the New Hampshire primary, as Lyndon Larouche – coincidentally another Rochester native – is again campaigning vigorously in the teeth of media indifference.)

Brushing aside Larouche, Rigazio said he wanted to be included in all New Hampshire debates along with political activist Al Sharpton, former U.S. Sen. Carol Moseley-Braun, U.S. Senators Joe Lieberman, John Kerry, John Edwards and Bob Graham, U.S. Representatives Richard Gephardt and Dennis Kucinich, and former Governor Howard Dean.

Rigazio feels he stands out from the pack because of his political platform. He is against federal tax cuts, he opposes unfair free world trade, he seeks a substantial hike in the minimum wage, and he would introduce a Canadian-style universal health-care system.

"I am very much against Bush's economic agenda. He is giving tax breaks and tax cuts when we have nothing but red ink," said Rigazio. "He, Reagan and Bush 1 have used one and a half trillion dollars of Social Security money. They raided Social Security and didn't tax people for it. With Clinton, we had false economic growth in the stock market which created a Social Security surplus. Bush 2 came in and gave away the surplus. Now the government owes Social Security $3 trillion, according to former Treasury Secretary Paul O'Neil," said Rigazio.

To redress the shortfall, Rigazio said he would increase employee and employer contributions of 6.2 percent each to 8 percent each.

"The money raised must be put in a special fund to be there for the baby boomers," Rigazio added, who is also adamantly opposed to privatization of Social Security.

On the economic front, Rigazio wants to take the United States out of the World Trade Organization. He asserts it was set up by multinational corporations "so that they can make their products anywhere and still have access to the U.S. market."

He also opposes Bush's recent tax cuts. "I don't believe they will create investment or create jobs," he said.

As an economic stimulus, Rigazio, if elected president, would increase the minimum wage by $2 an hour in 2005, hike it by a further $1 in 2006, and by another $1 in 2007, to bring it over the $9 per hour mark.

"That will lessen the demand on safety net programs," said Rigazio.

Turning to health issues, Rigazio advocates a Canadian-style health care program.

"Fifty million Americans don't have health coverage," he pointed out, while warning that a universal health-care system would inevitably be slower due to increased demand for treatment.

Regarding foreign policy, Rigazio noted that he supported the president in disarming Iraq.

"North Korea is not our problem. That should be dealt with by South Korea, Japan and China," he said.

Rigazio, who owns three retail stores in New Hampshire, said he will not solicit $1 for his presidential bid and won't accept donations.

"I expect to spend $100,000 of my own money," he said. "I would love to get 10 percent of the New Hampshire vote and send a message."

Rigazio insists that he should be included in the democratic presidential primary debates in this state.

"I am New Hampshire born and bred. A businessman should be able to run for the presidency of the United States. I should not be shut out of the debates. I want to be No. 10," he said.

Rigazio was born in Rochester in 1931, the son of Italian immigrants. He attended School Street School (founding an alumni association later in life) and graduated from Spaulding High School the year his father passed away.

Weathering hard times and enjoying good times in business, Rigazio extols the free enterprise system, and quotes his father, who said, "This is the land of opportunity, not the land of guarantee."

Rigazio is divorced with five children and seven grandchildren. He currently lives in Barrington.

He founded Signal Street Variety in 1985 with $12,000 working capital, and today, his stores have a combined annual turnover in excess of $15 million.

He is a past president of Rochester Lions Club, is a former member of Rochester Kiwanis, and belongs to Rochester Elks, American Legion Post 7 (he served for three years in the U.S. Army), and Rochester Rotary. He is also a member of NH Retail Grocers' Association.

He is currently Rochester Chamber of Commerce's Citizen of the Year, and is a strong supporter of many local causes, including Rochester Opera House.

He ran as a Democrat for the U.S. Congress in 1970, and took part in the 1992 U.S. Democratic Presidential Primary.

In the past, Rigazio has also supported John Anderson's American Party, Ross Perot's Reform Party, and has been a supporter of Pat Buchanan in the New Hampshire Republican Presidential Primary.

For many years he has authored a semi-regular newspaper column called *National Politics is Everybody's Business.*

7

PUBLISHED AUG. 11, 2003
FRONT PAGE INTERVIEW WITH MANCHESTER UNION LEADER
Reprinted courtesy of *The Manchester Union Leader*

TRADE ISSUES MOTIVATE LONG-SHOT RIGAZIO PRESIDENTIAL BID

Back in the race: The Democrat also ran in 1992

By RILEY YATES
UNION LEADER CORRESPONDENT

BARRINGTON – Leaving church recently, a fellow parishioner shouted to John D. Rigazio, "Hey, Mr. President."

It's true, the 72-year-old Barrington resident is running in New Hampshire's Democratic primary. But the comment didn't seem all that appropriate to Rigazio. To him it wasn't funny – at all.

"I pulled him aside and said, 'Look, I take my politics seriously and I'm trying to make a difference,'" Rigazio said Friday.

The parishioner wasn't the first to hit on the quixotic qualities of Rigazio's campaign. His five children are embarrassed by it and won't talk about it, he said. Friends and neighbors keep asking him why he's spending so much money on newspaper advertisements. State Democratic leaders won't even return his phone calls.

For Rigazio, the reason he's running is simple. Although he's expecting to spend up to $200,000 of his own money, he said it doesn't matter as long as he can get other candidates talking about the issues he believes must be addressed.

The No. 1 issue for Rigazio is free trade and America's participation in the World Trade Organization, a multinational trade governing body that can strike down tariffs passed by a country's elected officials.

The organization is hurting U.S. workers, Rigazio said, as big business moves its factories overseas to such places as China, where labor costs are miniscule compared to here. Rigazio said he wants America to pull out of it and work to preserve the manufacturing jobs that used to form the backbone of the country's wealth and prosperity.

If one of the major candidates would go on record for this, Rigazio said he would drop out of the race. Until then, he said he is hoping to use whatever voice he can muster to make people think about the issue, and others – like raising the minimum wage, and controlling the burgeoning cost of health care and the huge deficits that have been built in the past three years.

"If I could get six or eight or ten percent of the vote, it would really send a message in the primary," Rigazio said.

He said his Italian immigrant father taught him that America offered opportunity; anyone could take a shot at being great, even if it meant risking failure, he said.

It was in 1964 that Rigazio "lost his marbles," he said, by becoming interested in politics. Listening to Lyndon Johnson's Great Society inaugural address, Rigazio said he realized his country was going in a direction that didn't match the vision he had been raised with.

"It was contradicting what my father said. Johnson wanted America to be the land of guarantee, not opportunity," Rigazio said.

By this time, Rigazio was running a wholesale business out of Rochester that he'd taken charge of after his father died when he was only 17. Along the way, he was drafted as an infantryman in the Korean Conflict, serving for two years.

Rigazio said he began watching television news and reading several newspapers a day. He wanted answers to how America could spend so much money for social programs it couldn't afford, he said.

While living in Maine in 1970, he ran for Congress, losing to incumbent Peter M. Kyros by more than 13,000 votes. Later, he flirted with liberal Republican John B. Anderson's 1980 third-party presidential bid. In 1996, he supported Pat Buchanan, whose America-first stance he liked.

This time around, Rigazio said he doesn't think much of any of the candidates. And that's why he decided to run, as he also did in 1992. President Bush, he said, is the "worst and weakest President we've ever had," with his tax cuts being "cuckoo-crazy."

The Democratic candidates aren't doing all that much better, he said, especially in their criticism of the invasion and occupation of Iraq, which Rigazio said was necessary to ensure stability in the Middle East.

For his campaign, Rigazio isn't raising money like the rest of the candidates. His money comes instead from the lucrative stores he owns in Seabrook that cater mostly to Massachusetts residents crossing the border to buy cheap cigarettes and liquor.

Rigazio isn't holding political rallies either. And while he has a campaign office in Rochester, his main mode of reaching people is by buying newspaper ads in *The Union Leader, Foster's Daily Democrat* and *The Rochester Times.* Today an ad will be running in the *Des Moines Register* of Iowa.

Rigazio said he wants to be a part of any political debate held in New Hampshire. The perspective he would give would be so much different from everyone else's, he said.

"They always talk about hearing from the average person," Rigazio said. "And that's me."

At times though, Rigazio appears to dream a little about being not so average. Maybe he could get on one of the national cable networks, he said, and tell his ideas to the entire nation.

"If miracles upon miracles happened and I got some national exposure, I would name a vice presidential candidate," Rigazio said. "Or at least send him a letter."

8

PUBLISHED OCT. 18, 2003 IN FOSTER'S DAILY DEMOCRAT
Reprinted courtesy of John Nolan and *The Rochester Times*

CANDIDATE SWITCHES SIDES IN RACE

By JOHN NOLAN

ROCHESTER — After campaigning for several months as a Democratic candidate in New Hampshire's presidential primary, local businessman John Rigazio has registered as a Republican.

"I switched on Oct. 15," said the Barrington resident and owner of Signal Street Variety, explaining he is spending up to $200,000 of his own money in getting out his presidential message.

He will now file in Concord for the presidential primary Jan. 27.

"I really think it is better this way. I was not recognized from the get-go by the New Hampshire Democratic Party, and it seemed, for the most part, that the press ignored my candidacy and positions on issues," said Rigazio, adding that as a Republican, he will not bash President Bush.

This does not mean he agrees with Bush's policies, however.

"My big difference with Bush is that he is giving away American jobs, unfairly, to foreign countries, and he is still proclaiming free world trade," Rigazio said.

He also disagrees with the president's current policy in Iraq.

"He has run back to the United Nations," said Rigazio, who thinks the United States should take care of the situation by a redeployment of its own troops and by recouping much of the $87 billion in reconstruction costs from the subsequent sale of Iraqi oil.

Rigazio does not favor encouraging people to invest any part of Social Security in the stock market.

"I am totally opposed to (Social Security) privatization and I am totally opposed to Bush's tax cut — it won't create investment or jobs, it will add to the deficit," Rigazio said. "Bush has spent Social Security since the day he entered office. It is deceitful."

"Our health care system is so broken, it is unfixable. I am calling for a socialistic system like Canada, and maybe we can eliminate some of their flaws," Rigazio said.

"Bush has been raising all this money for his campaign from the big businesses he has been helping since he got elected. It is time to put the American economy No. 1 and the world economy second," Rigazio said.

"I realize the president will win the New Hampshire primary, but a vote for me will send a message to Washington (D.C.) that policies must change," he added.

Rigazio is in agreement with Democratic presidential candidate Dennis Kucinich, who is strongly advocating that the United States must get out of the World Trade Organization and the North American Free Trade Agreement.

"I am backing Dennis Kucinich on the Democratic side. My fiancée and I have already sent him $4,000," Rigazio said. "I hope to meet him to further his campaign."

Meanwhile, Rigazio continues to maintain his website, which has had more than 550 visitors since it was launched in July, and has a campaign headquarters on North Main Street.

9

THE FORMER WEBSITE:
Rigazio4President.com

John Donald Rigazio

REPUBLICAN PRESIDENTIAL CANDIDATE (2004)

LIFETIME BUSINESSMAN – WHOLESALE & RETAIL FOOD BUSINESS

My name is **John Donald Rigazio**. I was born in Rochester, NH, on August 18, 1931. I am running as a Democrat in NH's Presidential Primary. My name will be on the ballot for the office of **President of the United States**. Why? Because I have the **issues** and the **answers** to America's **greatest problems** which **threaten our national sovereignty** and **threaten** our country's authority to **control our own economic destiny.**

Please note:

I, John Donald Rigazio, have switched parties from the Democrat to the Republican party. I will be on the ballot on January 27th as a Republican. My issues and answers are the same as I have stated on this website.

I am asking Republicans to send President Bush a message by voting for me. I am also asking Democrats to vote for Dennis J. Kucinich who, like me, wants the U.S. to get out of the World Trade Organization. Thank you.

JOHN DONALD RIGAZIO

LIFETIME BUSINESSMAN – WHOLESALE & RETAIL FOOD BUSINESS

REPUBLICAN PRESIDENTIAL CANDIDATE (2004)

MY ISSUES

1. Fair world trade instead of unfair world trade.

2. Get out of the W.T.O. (World Trade Organization)

3. Try to cancel or rescind all of the Bush tax cuts for the rich and higher income.

4. Increase the minimum wage $2.00 per hour as soon as possible and add $1.00 per hour in the next two years.

5. Adopt the universal health care system of Canada (50 million Americans must have health care).

6. Change the welfare system drastically – no new babies to be put on welfare.

7. Do not privatize or semi-privatize the Social Security system.

8. Cut the interest rate another ½%. This will help fight recession.

9. Stick with our commitment in changing Iraq's government into a free, self-governed nation.

10. Do not get deeply into the North Korean problem. Let South Korea, Japan, China and the United Nations handle North Korea.

11. Provide federal government jobs like the old W.P.A. to welfare recipients to rebuild our infrastructure.

12. Make every American worker, citizen or not, pay into our Social Security System.

11

PUBLISHED JAN. 13, 2004

ONLY IN AMERICA AND ONLY IN NEW HAMPSHIRE

IF a retired businessman like myself is very worried in regards to the DIRECTION AMERICA IS HEADING and IF he CANNOT vote for the incumbent President or the nine Democratic presidential candidates, what option does that person have?

Well, he or she can go to the NH Secretary of State's office and plunk down $1,000 and be listed on NH's Jan. 27th FIRST IN THE NATION PRESIDENTIAL PRIMARY. WHAT BETTER WAY TO HAVE YOUR POLITICAL CONVICTIONS AIRED TO THE AMERICAN PUBLIC?

There are (including me) 14 people on the Republican primary ballot. Of course, the president is #1, but of the other 13, my $200,000 SELF-PAID campaign and my website is BY FAR THE STRONGEST IN REGARDS TO THE MAIN ISSUES (EXPORTING AMERICAN JOBS AND WINNING THE WAR IN IRAQ).

Besides the nine politicians running on the Democratic side of the ballot, there are 16 others on the NH first in the nation primary ballot.

EVERY FOUR YEARS THE EYES OF THE NATION ARE ON NEW HAMPSHIRE

HOWEVER, the two major political parties IGNORE ANYONE but the front runners and the national press only focuses on the Washington politicians presented by the two major parties.

In the past seven months I have placed political ads in the *NH Union Leader, Foster's Daily Democrat* and *The Rochester Times.* With the exception of *The Rochester Times* my HEAVILY FINANCED political newspaper ads with my MAIN ISSUES and ANSWERS HAVE BEEN ABSOLUTELY IGNORED.

DON'T LET THE POLITICAL PARTIES AND THE NATIONAL PRESS STOP YOU from voting for me, John Donald Rigazio.

Of course, President Bush is going to win the NH first in the nation Republican Primary; however, we could SEND HIM A MESSAGE by voting for John Donald Rigazio.

That message is we want to put OUR AMERICAN ECONOMY BEFORE THE WORLD ECONOMY and we must GET OUT of the WTO (World Trade Organization) IF WE WANT TO CONTROL OUR OWN ECONOMIC DESTINY.

Also, we must deploy 40,000 plus troops from South Korea and Germany to Iraq to win the guerilla war which is our MOST VITAL INTEREST IN OUR WAR AGAINST WORLD-WIDE TERRORISM.

We CANNOT continue being the "Policemen of the World." Let South Korea and Europe put THEIR OWN GROUND TROOPS IN THEIR OWN COUNTRY.

P.S. About 12 years ago, I had four 17-year-old Danish students staying at my house. We shared a joke about the glass being half full or half empty.

Christian then asked me if he could tell a joke, and of course, I said yes. The joke was about NH presidential primaries: One NH citizen asked his neighbor who he was going to vote for, and his neighbor said, "I don't know. I only met Dukakis three times."

12

I HAVE THE ISSUES AND THE ANSWERS

#1 ISSUE: IRAQ AND AFGHANISTAN

We have well over 40,000 GROUND TROOPS in South Korea and Germany which should be RE-DEPLOYED to Iraq and Afghanistan IMMEDIATELY. Their MISSION will be to SECURE THE BORDERS of Iraq and Afghanistan from INFILTRATION OF TERRORISTS and to SECURE THE OIL PIPELINES FROM SABOTAGE.

When they have secured the borders and oil pipelines, some troops then can JOIN OUR EXISTING FORCES to go on the OFFENSIVE TO ROOT OUT ALL THE EXISTING TERRORISTS in Iraq and Afghanistan.

Border security is A MUST to stop the guerilla warfare now taking place in Iraq and Afghanistan. Security of the oil pipelines IS A MUST if we expect the Iraq economy to prosper and if we expect to RECOUP SOME OF THE BILLIONS OF DOLLARS the U.S. will be spending to rebuild Iraq.

When we silence the guerilla warfare in Iraq and Afghanistan and install a freely elected government in both Iraq and Afghanistan, the U.S. can then take the MAJORITY OF OUR TROOPS HOME.

We must let the UNITED NATIONS handle the NORTH KOREA AND IRAN THREATS. The U.S. can be PART OF the United Nations' decisions on what to do in North Korea and Iran BUT the U.S. CANNOT GO IT ALONE like we HAD TO DO IN IRAQ.

#2 ISSUE IS UNFAIR TRADE

America needs a new agency like the homeland security to STABILIZE and REBUILD our economy. We must pass laws which stop foreign countries and large worldwide corporations from UNFAIRLY taking American jobs from our country.

Not only should the new agency stabilize our manufacturing jobs and our hi-tech jobs, but they must protect all American jobs from unfair competition and stupid laws like Senate Bill S722 and of course cancel B1 Visa and L1 Visa Bills. In my opinion, Senate Bill S722 is like closing down McDonald's to fight obesity in America.

THERE WASN'T ANY PRESS AT MY PRESS CONFERENCE ON SEPT. 4TH, HOWEVER, I DID TALK TO PAUL HARRINGTON, WHO GAVE ME THIS INFORMATION ON S722:

There is a very dangerous Senate Bill (S722) sponsored by Senator Richard Durbin (D-Illinois); recent co-sponsors are Senator Hillary Clinton (D-NY), Senator Charles Schumer (D-NY) and Senator Diane Feinstein (D-CA). S722 WILL NOT ONLY HURT OUR ECONOMY IT WILL PREVENT MILLIONS OF SMALL BUSINESS OWNERS FROM SELLING THEIR PRODUCTS. This bill (S722) is intended to amend the Federal Food Drug and Cosmetic Act (FDCA) and shake the foundation of the Dietary Supplement Health and Education Act (DSHEA).

This month's issue of *Fortune Magazine* (August 2003), titled "The Power Issue," just happens to have a 19-page Special Advertising Section. The first page says, "Corporate America's New Sales Force" then it goes on to say: DESPITE THE SPUTTERING ECONOMY, independent contractors are re-energizing the U.S. retail industry through the art of direct selling. The next page states: The direct-selling industry, with U.S. sales of nearly $28 billion, is exploding. It has become a magnet for corporate behemoths and entrepreneurs.

This bill (S722) should drastically hurt many of the companies mentioned in this issue of *Fortune*. S722 will also take away OUR FREEDOM OF WHAT WE AS INDIVIDUAL CITIZENS WANT TO USE FOR DIETARY SUPPLEMENTS. Please join me and many others to stop this insane form of legislation.

Sincerely,

Rep. Paul Harrington District 60 – Nashua, New Hampshire

So America's NEW AGENCY to STABILIZE and REBUILD must be able to PASS LAWS AND ENFORCE LAWS to keep America from becoming a SERVICE INDUSTRY ECONOMY.

#3 ISSUE: GET OUT OF THE WTO

Unless America gets out of the WTO (World Trade Organization) we WILL NOT BE ABLE TO CONTROL OUR OWN ECONOMIC DESTINY.

"The WTO is a WEALTH TRANSFER ORGANIZATION, HEAVILY WEIGHTED AGAINST U.S. INTERESTS, and the TRAGIC FLAW IN FREE WORLD TRADE IS THAT ONLY AMERICA PRACTICES IT."

I HAVE OTHER ISSUES WHICH I WILL PUT FORWARD IN MY NEXT POLITICAL COLUMN.

13

PUBLISHED OCT. 26, 2003

THE UNITED STATES IS LOSING THE WAR IN IRAQ

I CANNOT BELIEVE the Bush Administration was so naïve (OR DUMB) to think the war in Iraq WAS OVER IN MAY of this year when in fact the war was JUST BEGINNING.

In early June I called for 40,000 U.S. troops from South Korea and Germany to be redeployed to Iraq to secure the borders of Iraq, guard the oil pipelines and go on the offensive to root out all the terrorists in Iraq.

Terrorists are slipping into Iraq on a daily basis, and with many of Saddam's loyalists are killing and wounding U.S. servicemen. They are also sabotaging oil pipelines and killing and wounding Iraqi people who are trying to provide Iraq with a new police force, new army, and a new government.

MAKE NO MISTAKE about it, the terrorists ARE WINNING THE GUERILLA WARFARE IN IRAQ. Unless the United States sends 40 to 50 thousand more U.S. troops to Iraq we, in a year or two, WILL HAVE TO PULL OUT OF IRAQ.

Of course, this will mean AFGHANISTAN WILL ALSO, IN A FEW YEARS, FALL TO THE TERRORISTS.

This will leave our main Democratic ally, ISRAEL, to try to SURVIVE in the Mideast while SURROUNDED BY TERRORISTS with NO ALLIES in Iraq and Afghanistan.

OUR VITAL INTEREST IS IN IRAQ.

World War II and the Korean War have been over for 50 years. The United States has made both Germany and South Korea economic super powers who CAN and SHOULD protect their own countries with their own foot soldiers.

OUR VITAL INTEREST IS IN IRAQ. We have U.S. TROOPS IN HARM'S WAY while the U.S. government looks for MERCENARY SOLDIERS to FINISH THE GROUND WAR WHICH WE STARTED.

Yes, 87 billion is a lot of money, HOWEVER, leaving American troops in Iraq to be picked off like sitting ducks is something I just CANNOT STOMACH.

JOHN DONALD RIGAZIO SAYS ...

To hell with the U.N., who WON'T SEND ANY TROOPS to Iraq, WON'T SEND ANY MONEY to rebuild Iraq, and if they had lived up to their duty to ENFORCE IRAQ'S BREAKING OF U.N. LAWS FOR THE PAST 12 YEARS WE WOULD NOT HAVE HAD TO DISARM SADDAM HUSSEIN BY OURSELVES.

The United Nations should COME OUT OF THE CLOSET and DEAL WITH NORTH KOREA DIRECTLY. Americans should be PART OF THE UNITED NATIONS' DECISIONS IN NORTH KOREA.

I think the Bush Administration's decision TO CUT THE NUMBER OF our troops in Iraq ONLY ENDANGERS THE EXISTING TROOPS MORE and will, in a few years, LOSE THE WAR IN IRAQ and ALSO LOSE AFGHANISTAN.

We started the war, let's deploy 40 to 50 thousand U.S. troops from South Korea and Germany and WIN the war in Iraq.

14

PUBLISHED AUG. 14, 2003

BUSH FEDERAL DEFICITS THREATEN SOCIAL SECURITY

The United States FISCAL YEAR ends on SEPT. 30th for this year's 2003 figures.

OUR GOVERNMENT announced several weeks ago that the BUDGET DEFICIT for the YEAR END 9/30/03 was going to be $455 BILLION.

I AM REPRINTING A 7/21/03 LETTER TO THE EDITOR

Budget-deficit picture full of 'gimmicks'

USA Today gave the story about the soaring government deficit the coverage it deserves by putting it on the front page. But the newspaper fell for the Bush administration gimmick to understate the red ink ("Deficit soars to $455B," News, Wednesday).

On page one of the administration's budget report, officials say the deficit will be $455 billion this year. But on page 57 of the same report, they say it actually will reach a mind-boggling $698 billion.

By looting Social Security and other trust funds, George W. Bush makes the page-one figure look lower, but he breaks his promise that Social Security money be used for that purpose only.

USA Today also failed to mention that deficits like these will cause the government to pile up $3.6 trillion in debt in just the next five years. Twenty years from now, when soldiers who fought in Iraq are looking for military retiree checks and baby boomers are looking for Social Security checks, we'll have to tell them: "Whoops! The money is not there. Mr. Bush never accounted for the money he borrowed from the trust funds as a liability and gave it out as tax cuts."

The press has to stop falling for the gimmicks, or America's creditworthiness will go the way of Enron.

Sen. Ernest F. Hollings, D-S.C.
Washington

SO the Bush administration's $455 BILLION deficit is REALLY $698 BILLION. Plus we have THREE MONTHS LEFT in the 9/30/03 fiscal year where Iraq spending will have to be accounted for, the U.S. government has three more months to steal the Social Security surplus, and the July, August and September expected revenues will have GREAT REVENUE SHORTFALLS.

1 TRILLION DOLLAR DEFICIT

The ACTUAL DEFICIT for this year end 9/30/03 WILL NOT BE $455 BILLION BUT $1 TRILLION.

With our government raiding the Social Security trust fund, with the costs of the war in Iraq, and with the REVENUE SHORTFALLS it will be $1 TRILLION.

When our government reported that this year's 9/30/03 federal deficit was $455 billion they said the 9/30/04 deficit was going to be $475 billion.

GEORGE W. BUSH'S (2004 BUDGET) YEAR END 9/30/04

The president's 2004 budget is our expansionary budget. By that I mean his proposed $2.2 trillion IN SPENDING (which doesn't include the expense in Iraq) is $304 billion MORE THAN OUR TOTAL FEDERAL REVENUES RECEIVED THE PREVIOUS YEAR.

It is of my businessman's VIEWPOINT that revenues for year ending 9/30/04 will be $500 to $600 BILLION LESS THAN THE PREVIOUS YEAR'S REVENUES. Of course, the $2.2 trillion in spending could be $2.5 trillion. The REASON THE REVENUES will be down is that BUSINESS PROFITS AND PERSONAL INCOME WILL BE WAY DOWN, thus we will have a $500 TO $600 BILLION REVENUE SHORTFALL.

So it is of my opinion that the (2004) budget could not only be the projected $304 billion recognized in the EXPANSIONARY BUDGET but could reach nearly $1 trillion.

2003 AND 2004 FEDERAL DEFICITS THREATEN THE SOCIAL SECURITY PROGRAM AS WE KNOW IT TODAY.

The president wants to REFORM (semi-privatize) the Social Security system in order to get out of the $3 trillion that our government owes the Social Security program.

This $3 trillion our government owes the Social Security Trust Fund is (ACCORDING TO FORMER SECRETARY OF THE TREASURY PAUL O'NEIL)

NOT EVEN ACCOUNTED FOR in the FEDERAL BOOKS. I guess if WE OWE IT TO OURSELVES it is a NON-ENTRY IN THE BOOKS.

THE FEDERAL GOVERNMENT IS NOT GOING TO REPAY THE SOCIAL SECURITY SURPLUS, SO I, JOHN DONALD RIGAZIO, REPUBLICAN CANDIDATE FOR PRESIDENT, HAVE THE ANSWER TO KEEPING SOCIAL SECURITY INTACT.

(Step #1) In 2005, put ALL Social Security revenue into a SPECIAL SOCIAL SECURITY ACCOUNT which the U.S. government CAN NOT use for any other purpose.

(Step #2) Unfortunately, we must increase workers' Social Security payments from 6.2% of their income to 8%. This, of course, means the EMPLOYERS' MATCHING SOCIAL SECURITY PAYMENTS also go up from 6.2% to 8%.

So in 2005 the Social Security payments from the workers is 8% and a matching 8% is now 16% compared to the 6.2% + 6.2% which equals 12.4%.

This increase of 3.6% will soon start generating a huge SOCIAL SECURITY SURPLUS.

(Step #3) We must INCREASE THE BASE of American workers who pay Social Security. I propose EVERY AMERICAN WORKER, CITIZEN OR NOT, must PAY INTO and receive Social Security when they become eligible.

IF the BUSH REPUBLICAN ADMINISTRATION LETS ANY YOUNG OR OLD AMERICAN WORKER TAKE ANY OF THEIR SOCIAL SECURITY PAYMENTS OUT OF THE GENERAL SOCIAL SECURITY POT, IT'S THE FIRST STEP TOWARD DISMANTLING THE CURRENT GOVERNMENT GUARANTEED SOCIAL SECURITY SYSTEM.

15

PUBLISHED NOV. 9, 2003

PRESIDENT BUSH DOES NOT DESERVE A SECOND TERM

On Tuesday, Jan. 27, my name, John Donald Rigazio, will appear on the Republican side of NH's first in the nation presidential primary. Please check my website and you will read that I am indeed a serious candidate.

Upon taking office, President Bush gave us Americans a tax cut from the SURPLUS OF OUR SOCIAL SECURITY SYSTEM. As we proceed into November, the Bush administration IS WORKING on legislation to PRIVATIZE or at the very least SEMI-PRIVATIZE THE SOCIAL SECURITY SYSTEM. This legislation will SEVERELY DISMANTLE the Social Security system AS WE KNOW IT TODAY.

If anyone checks my website and pulls up my political ad "Bush deficits threaten Social Security," they will get an IN-DEPTH PICTURE of what he intends to do to the current Social Security system which, if left alone, HAS SUFFICIENT FUNDING TO PRESERVE OUR CURRENT SOCIAL SECURITY PROGRAM.

President Bush also IS IN FULL AGREEMENT WITH THE WTO (World Trade Organization). This organization (in which we have ONE VOTE, along with every other country in the world) is a WEALTH TRANSFER ORGANIZATION with INTERESTS HEAVILY WEIGHTED AGAINST THE UNITED STATES, AND THE TERRIBLE FLAW IN FREE WORLD TRADE IS THAT ONLY AMERICA PRACTICES IT.

America CANNOT CONTROL ITS OWN ECONOMIC DESTINY while a member of the WTO. ONLY MYSELF, now a REPUBLICAN candidate for president, and Democratic candidate for president Dennis J. Kucinich are for getting out of the WTO.

We now have steel tariffs on foreign steel which is stabilizing our steel industry (over 30 U.S. steel companies went bankrupt in the past few years). Guess what? On July 12 the WTO RULED OUR TARIFFS ILLEGAL and we are appealing that decision in which the WTO law OVERRULED OUR LAW.

UNFAIR world trade WAS MY MAIN ISSUE; however, the Bush Administration's handling of Phase II of the Iraq War is now our #1 problem.

The president is trying to BEG and BUY OFF, WITH FAVORABLE ECONOMIC TRADE POLICIES, foreign countries to send troops to Iraq to fight in the guerilla war that we started.

WHY THE PRESIDENT DOES NOT DEPLOY 40,000 OF OUR OWN TROOPS IN SOUTH KOREA AND GERMANY TO WIN THIS GUERILLA WAR IN IRAQ IS BEYOND ME.

I guess it is NOT POLITICALLY POPULAR to send more U.S. troops to Iraq when most Americans want our troops home.

This Iraq War (as I see it) has shades of Vietnam written all over it. I feel we lost thousands of U.S. servicemen in Vietnam while trying to TRAIN A SOUTH VIETNAMESE ARMY to fight North Vietnam SO WE COULD BRING OUR TROOPS HOME.

NOW IN IRAQ they are giving us the SAME BULL. We must train the Iraqi police force and NEW IRAQI ARMY to fight the guerilla war now being carried on with Saddam's loyalists and TERRORIST GROUPS FROM ALL OVER THE MIDDLE EAST.

THIS IS NOT GOING TO WORK

Please read on my website my last two political advertisements: WE ARE LOSING THE WAR IN IRAQ and my newest article, HOW TO WIN THE WAR IN IRAQ, AND MOST IMPORTANTLY, HOW TO BRING THE MAJORITY OF OUR TROOPS HOME.

GIVING ME YOUR VOTE ON JAN. 27

This will send them a message in Washington.

1. The Social Security system is NOT BROKE and doesn't need fixing.

2. We need a new agency called Homeland Security for our economy, which has the power to make NEW trade laws and REVERSE some OLD TRADE AGREEMENTS. Of course, TO ENFORCE OUR OWN UNITED STATES TRADE LAWS we must GET OUT OF THE WTO.

3. We must deploy our troops from SOUTH KOREA and GERMANY TO WIN THE GUERILLA WAR IN IRAQ, WHICH WILL BE A MAJOR VICTORY IN THE WAR AGAINST WORLDWIDE TERRORISTS.

16

PUBLISHED JUNE 14, 2003

HOW TO FIX THE WELFARE SYSTEM

Whereas NH is currently working to meet the federal goals of welfare-to-work, and whereas a 20-year-old woman in the South is expecting her THIRD set of twins while on welfare, I am asking *The Rochester Times* and *Foster's* to publish my view on the current welfare system.

I did pay for this column at my own expense, but now that I am retired I can't afford it.

I thank you for your consideration.

(This is a repeat of a political column I wrote on Aug. 6, 2001.)

What prompted me to write this column is a newspaper editorial from *The American Press,* Lake Charles, La. I have, at my own expense, reprinted this editorial which was in the Sunday, July 15 *Foster's.*

What other papers have said; no quick fix for welfare

It seemed so simple. Get work or get off welfare. Congress passed the law, President Clinton signed it ... Three years after the most comprehensive welfare reform in U.S. history, the structure is threatening to fall apart.

We're learning that it may take as long to solve a major social problem as it did for that problem to develop. That's a revelation politicians don't want to hear in an era of quick fixes designed to get instant voter approval.

Family heads who found jobs – on threat of losing welfare payments – are having just as much trouble paying for food, rent and utilities as those who remained on the welfare rolls, according to a national survey.

And ordering people to go to work doesn't mean it will happen. The survey of families either on welfare or just departed from welfare shows that major obstacles face people with little education or work skills when they apply for a job.

They either get no jobs at all or they get the lowest-paid, most menial jobs. And the majority of those menial jobs are the kind that don't allow for growth or development of skills. ...

What we've got is a welfare reform program designed to produce immediate success aimed at a problem in which expectations of immediate success are totally unrealistic.

Poverty, illiteracy and social disadvantages were generations in the making. It will probably take generations to erase those disadvantages.

The kind of education that will lift people out of poverty takes years to acquire for the first generation alone, and it takes another 16 years for the second generation to follow in the footsteps of the first.

It can be done – with time, patience and a lasting sense of responsibility.

American Press
Lake Charles, La.

THE GET WORK OR GET OFF WELFARE BILL PASSED BY CONGRESS THREE YEARS AGO WAS DESTINED FOR FAILURE

Three years ago when this comprehensive welfare reform bill was passed I wrote letters and told everyone who would listen to me that this bill would not work.

There are two major reasons why this new three-year MAJOR welfare reform bill did not work. The FIRST is that it did not apply ANY REAL INCENTIVES for a person or family to get off welfare and join the workforce at a minimum wage with no health care benefits.

The UNSECURED wages that a welfare recipient would receive FOR WORKING compared with the SECURED welfare payments plus welfare benefits they would lose provided no incentive for a welfare recipient to get a job and get off welfare.

There has got to be a greater difference in what Americans get FOR WORKING as opposed to what welfare gives them for NOT WORKING.

I think the national minimum wage should be increased by at least $3 per hour and that America's lower income (working poor) SHOULD be given the same health and dental care benefits provided to welfare recipients.

The second reason the three-year welfare reform bill did not work is ...

The American welfare system is BREEDING welfare families in America. Like it or not, realize it or not, welfare in America has become a standard of living for many American poor families.

In many cases the secured welfare income and benefits are better than the unsecured income of the working poor with no benefits. It's little wonder why MANY children brought into this world in a welfare family will at child bearing ages become the household head of a NEW WELFARE FAMILY.

THE WELFARE SYSTEM NEEDS TO CHANGE

I believe it is NOT ONLY the moral obligation of a mother and father to LOVE their newborn BABY BUT it is also THEIR DUTY to PROVIDE for that baby. So as of January of 2003 NO NEW BABIES can be ADDED TO THE WELFARE rolls.

If the mother and father, or the mother and HER immediate family, cannot provide for their newborn they must surrender it to a STATE OR FEDERAL run orphanage.

This orphanage for newborns whose parents cannot provide for them could be minimally staffed and maximum staffed with senior citizen volunteers.

In this orphanage the baby IN MOST CASES will get better care than it would get by being added to the welfare ranks.

Is an orphanage cruel and unusual punishment for a newborn baby? I don't think so. Most of the babies born into welfare have two STRIKES against them and society has three strikes against them.

The mother and father and immediate family who CANNOT PROVIDE for their newborn will have to TEMPORARILY put THE NEWBORN into a state-run orphanage. THEY CAN VISIT THEIR BABY on a daily basis. The new mother and father CAN TAKE their newborn from the orphanage WHEN they can prove they can provide for them.

I don't feel there will be many newborns surrendered to the state-run orphanages; however, we must have a place for the baby IF the new mother and father CANNOT PROVIDE FOR IT.

WE MUST STOP BREEDING WELFARE FAMILIES

If a current welfare family CANNOT get a new baby ADDED ON THE WELFARE ROLLS and if an unwed teenage mother CANNOT START A NEW

WELFARE FAMILY then the number on welfare is sure to SHRINK YEAR AFTER YEAR. Why should welfare families continue to have babies and WHY should their teenagers create new welfare families when many working families wait to have a family until they can afford it OR have one or two children because they can't afford any more?

I LIVED IN ROCHESTER, NH when I wrote about TRUE welfare reform and my solution which was similar to this letter. A Rochester resident, "Diane Sharkey," chastised me for my proposal of taking a baby away from its mother and PLACING it in an orphanage. This was HER OPINION, which is fine, but SHE said I owned variety stores and PROBABLY gave my customers beer and cigarettes for food stamps.

I didn't comment on Ms. Sharkey's letter then, HOWEVER, I do NOT NOW or EVER HAVE BEEN AUTHORIZED TO ACCEPT FOOD STAMPS. I never did apply for them because I know food stamp recipients can get more for the food stamps at the supermarkets.

ANYHOW, I AM GOING TO SEND THIS COLUMN TO *THE AMERICAN PRESS* **IN LAKE CHARLES, LA.**

THEIR SOLUTION, like many other intellectuals, is BETTER EDUCATION FOR ALL WILL EVENTUALLY WIPE OUT POVERTY IN AMERICA.

I believe that better education will help SOME get off welfare but the welfare system needs a major OVERHAULING if we are going to get the majority of American families off welfare and join America's lower income (WORKING POOR).

17

PUBLISHED MAY 6, 2003

HOW TO FIX AMERICA'S AILING HEALTH CARE SYSTEM

To quote Dear Abby: "If it ain't broke, don't fix it." Well, it SURE AS HECK is broke.

We have a SEMI-SOCIALISTIC health care program which is serving fewer and fewer Americans at a higher and higher cost each year.

We have 40 million Americans with NO HEALTH INSURANCE and probably another 40 million who will lose their health insurance as it becomes TOO EXPENSIVE for their employers to pay for the EVER-INCREASING health care costs.

WE MUST SEGREGATE THE AMERICAN HEALTH CARE SYSTEM INTO THREE TIERS.

FIRST TIER

This is easy. It's called the free enterprise system. The patient pays all his own bills personally. The doctors and hospitals charge their patients directly.

NO GOVERNMENT money is involved and, of course, no government intervention between patient and caregiver.

Of course, the first tier free enterprise health care system will provide fast and best of care treatment. The caregivers will have to compete with each other in regards to prices charged their first tier patients.

SECOND TIER

I call this tier the semi-socialistic part of America's health care system. Medicare, veterans' benefits, Congressional health care benefits, etc.

EVERY HEALTH CARE GROUP that the federal and state taxpayers subsidized in any way, shape or manner must be put into the semi-socialistic tier two group.

This tier two group must have the government SET THE PRICES charged by all doctors, hospitals and most importantly, make the drug companies COMPETE IN PRICE for all the drugs used in America's semi-socialistic tier two health care system.

35

In the tier two system, all doctors must get a second opinion before an operation is to be performed. Of course, if an emergency operation is needed, the second option must be waived.

So IF any patient has taxpayers' money for his health care plan, they must go through the government's tier two health care plan.

The government would be the first payer and the patient's insurance company or HMO would be the second payer.

Would the health care service in the semi-socialistic tier two be as fast as the free enterprise tier one health care plan? Of course not, but the tier two health care plan MUST HAVE government regulations (and yes, red tape) to HELP KEEP COSTS DOWN. ESPECIALLY THE SKYROCKETING DRUG PRESCRIPTION PRICES.

THIRD TIER

The health care of all welfare recipients, all of America's working poor and other special case patients, get free medical attention from the U.S. government.

Our government must open new health care facilities for all Americans who cannot afford their own insurance.

Each state must have at least one or more federally run hospital to care for the poor and their families. The government can reopen air bases, naval bases and Army bases for hospitals for the poor.

The government could give doctors and new interns tax credit for working at one of these hospitals for the poor. The government could ask for senior citizen volunteers, etc., to keep costs down; retired doctors and nurses could also help.

Of course, all patient care in these health care facilities would be paid for by the government, so the government would have to control all the costs.

This tier three is a totally SOCIALISTIC HEALTH CARE PROGRAM and will probably render much slower health care. However, SLOW health care is better than NO health care at all.

THE ABOVE POLITICAL COLUMN ON HEALTH CARE
WAS IN THE AUG. 30, 2001, *FOSTERS.*

After re-reading it today, I think my three tier health care solution is a little too ambiguous, to say the least. However, our health care system has to change.

We probably now have close to 50 million Americans not covered by medical insurance, and the number of uninsured is growing every day.

The totally SOCIALISTIC HEALTH CARE SYSTEM (like Canada) is not perfect but it covers everybody.

I AM REPRINTING THIS LETTER TO THE EDITOR written several years ago by a doctor.

Single payer only way to save U.S. health care

To the Editors:

While I greatly respect both former Sen. Bill Bradley and Vice President Al Gore, neither of their health plans take into account what we know about how to achieve universal coverage at an affordable price.

What makes our system so expensive is we pay out 30 percent of our funds to cover the overhead expenses generated by the multiple insurance companies that administer HMOs. We know from our neighbors to the north this figure can be reduced to 10 percent with a single payer system that cuts out all the middle men.

By using a single payer system, Canada has been able to insure all its citizens at a cost that is less than what we are paying for a system that leaves 40 million people without insurance. Furthermore, their system allows consumers free choice of provider and physicians to decide what is "medically necessary" rather than some bureaucrat.

Why is it we keep coming up with these expensive and inadequate schemes when a cheaper and better model exists right next door? Is it because the insurance companies are poised with millions of dollars ready to put out another "Harry and Louise" media blitz of misinformation? You draw your own conclusions.

Dr. R.W. Chamberlin
Canterbury

While the Canadian health care system has a lot to be desired it will INCLUDE 50 million Americans who do not have any medical coverage.

18

PUBLISHED AUG. 9, 2007

2005 BANKRUPTCY LAW MUST BE REPEALED

The free enterprise system is so simple. You invest money into a business to get a return on your investment. This is called a PROFIT.

However, in the free enterprise system there is always the RISK of losing money on your investment. Take away the RISK and the free enterprise system changes from allowing investors the OPPORTUNITY to make a profit and becomes a GUARANTEE to make a profit.

The credit card companies are businesses which issue credit to just about anyone, regardless of the RISK. They render late charge fees of about 20 percent. They force many Americans into personal bankruptcy.

Up until 2005, a person who declared Chapter 7 personal bankruptcy could write off his or her credit card debt. That's the way it should be. However, in 2005 the credit card companies and their lobbyists got the U.S. Congress to pass the Bankruptcy Abuse Prevention and Consumer Protection Act of 2005.

This 2005 bill takes away the RISKS of the banking institutions who issue credit cards. The banks are secured creditors in a bankruptcy, which means a person declaring bankruptcy must still be liable for the full amount of his or her credit card debt.

We must amend or repeal the Bankruptcy Abuse Prevention and Consumer Protection Act of 2005.

When banks can no longer follow credit card debtors to the grave, they will think twice before they force debtors into bankruptcy with outrageous practices and charges.

In 2005, I wrote letters to the editor saying that the U.S. Congress should not pass this new 2005 bankruptcy bill, as it took the RISK away from the credit card companies and that was violating the rules of America's free enterprise system.

19

PUBLISHED DEC. 20, 2007

YOU CAN'T GET BLOOD OUT OF A TURNIP

I would like to republish my Aug. 9 letter to the editor.

2005 bankruptcy law must be repealed

The free enterprise system is so simple. You invest money into a business to get a return on your investment. This is called a PROFIT.

However, in the free enterprise system there is always the RISK of losing money on your investment. Take away the RISK and the free enterprise system changes from allowing investors the OPPORTUNITY to make a profit and becomes a GUARANTEE to make a profit.

The credit card companies are businesses which issue credit to just about anyone, regardless of the RISK. They render late charge fees of about 20 percent. They force many Americans into personal bankruptcy.

Up until 2005, a person who declared Chapter 7 personal bankruptcy could write off his or her credit card debt. That's the way it should be. However, in 2005 the credit card companies and their lobbyists got the U.S. Congress to pass the Bankruptcy Abuse Prevention and Consumer Protection Act of 2005.

This 2005 bill takes away the RISKS of the banking institutions who issue credit cards. The banks are secured creditors in a bankruptcy, which means a person declaring bankruptcy must still be liable for the full amount of his or her credit card debt.

We must amend or repeal the Bankruptcy Abuse Prevention and Consumer Protection Act of 2005.

When banks can no longer follow credit card debtors to the grave, they will think twice before they force debtors into bankruptcy with outrageous practices and charges.

In 2005, I wrote letters to the editor saying that the U.S. Congress should not pass this new 2005 bankruptcy bill, as it took the RISK away from the credit card companies and that was violating the rules of America's free enterprise system.

John Rigazio, Barrington

The biggest secret now being held back from the American public is large banks and credit card issuers are carrying the $900 billion plus of credit card default on the balance sheets as ASSETS.

The truth of the matter is these assets cannot be sold or borrowed upon. So in essence, these assets are really liabilities. That's why banks and credit card issuers are trying to extort money from any credit card holder to finance the bad debt credit card money on their books. Serves them right for trying to screw with the free enterprise system. Risk is needed to have the free enterprise system function correctly. Take away the risk and we have the malfunction result of $900 billion on the balance sheet of big banks and credit card issuers.

In case any reader can't correlate the heading of this letter, "You can't get blood out a turnip" means no way can the banks collect this $900 billion bad debt from the credit card holders who the credit card companies gave this $900 billion credit to. Why? They haven't got it.

20

PUBLISHED NOV. 29, 2007

IT'S THE ECONOMY, STUPID

Since George W. Bush became president, we in America have had a false economy propelled by government deficit spending and consumer deficit spending.

We must take some drastic measures before our dollar goes into free-fall and our current recession becomes a depression for many American families who are in debt or living paycheck to paycheck.

Like many Americans whose credit cards are all maxed out, the U.S. government has just about maxed out our credit from our lenders (foreign countries). The only reason foreign countries keep lending us billions (and in some cases trillions) of dollars is that they want to continue milking the American economy of our good jobs and extract money from the U.S. economy with their imbalance of trade with America.

So the trade imbalance with major foreign countries such as China, Japan, Europe, South Korea, and a few other oil rich small countries cannot be allowed to continue.

It won't happen in Bush's last year in office, but as soon as the next president takes office the new administration must tell the American people and the world that we must cancel and review all trade agreements; we can no longer provide good jobs to foreign countries at the expense of the American economy.

We must get out of the WTO, (World Trade Organization) which billionaire Wilbur E. Ross four years ago called "a wealth transfer organization, heavily weighted against the best interests of America, and the problem with free world trade is that only America practices it."

We must tell all of our trading partners that we still want free trade; however, it must be fair trade.

Our new trade agreements must have reciprocal and enforced trade policies which give job security to Americans in our own economy – is that too much to ask?

Now for all the foreign countries who are holding billions of American dollars – our government must let them invest in America; however, we must freeze our treasury notes owed to foreign countries and let them withdraw 10 percent a year of the treasury notes we owe them (of course they still make interest off the 90 percent of treasury notes we froze).

America is still the largest economy in the world by far and our trading partners, such as China, need us as much as we need them. America must balance our budget and start to pay down our debt. We cannot do this with the unfair trade agreements we now have.

The greatest crime in America will happen when many Americans with savings accounts, stocks, municipal and federal bonds, 401k's, pension funds and other assets are frozen by a world financial crisis.

I say it's better for America to balance our budget, control our own economic destiny and freeze the foreign countries' treasury notes that they bought from us while they made this money with unfair trade agreements.

This letter contains heavy stuff which should be brought up in the current presidential debate. Congressman Dennis Kucinich is the only candidate running for president who wants to get out of the WTO, rescind NAFTA and other unfair trade agreements. He has my vote.

Also replacing the IRS with the Fair Tax federal consumption tax will level the playing field with foreign countries whose workers receive $1 or $2 an hour. This Fair Tax will increase U.S. government revenues tremendously.

21

PUBLISHED JAN. 17, 2008

NOTHING HAS CHANGED

Four years ago in the NH Republican Primary, I ran for President of the U.S. Although President Bush had no major Republican opposition, there still was a Republican Primary.

Myself and 12 others were on the ballot. I spent a considerable amount of my own money and had a very impressive website. Three of us got a little over 1,000 votes, far more than the other 10 on the ballot. President Bush got 53,000. My main issue then was that "free world trade" was "unfair world trade." As billionaire Wilbur E. Ross so aptly put it, "The World Trade Organization (WTO) is a wealth transfer organization, heavily weighted against the U.S. And the problem with free world trade is only the U.S. practices it."

It is now four years past the 2004 NH Primary, and we still do not have fair world trade. Plus the fact that big business has invested billions in Communist Vietnam to tap in on their slave labor workforce, who work for much less than $1 per hour.

Anyone who thinks we in America are engaging in free world trade ought to run out and have their heads examined. They should then use their common sense and realize that America cannot compete with nations that employ slave labor.

Educated American citizens who say they are for free world trade and they are not protectionist make me want to vomit.

We don't have free world trade, and that will become a major issue as our economy continues to lose good jobs in our march toward a full blown recession.

22

PUBLISHED APRIL 30, 2007

DEFICITS DO MATTER

People are only interested in the small part of the economic puzzle which affects them immediately and directly.

The Republican Party, since Reagan, Bush Sr. and George W. Bush, have told the public what they want to hear, plus they not only pledge no new taxes but they, under George W. in particular, are in the process of huge tax cuts.

So, Americans, wake up. There is no free lunch. If we as a nation do not balance our budget, we will keep raising our national debt and increase the interest we have to pay on the deficits.

In the 2005 fiscal year, we paid $327 billion in interest, and in the fiscal year of 2006 we paid $360 billion in interest, mostly to foreign countries.

So the Republicans say the Democrats will raise your taxes if elected, but they continue to increase our national debt and increase our yearly interest payments.

In my opinion, the Republican administration under George W. Bush is like a CEO and we the American people are the shareholders. He is borrowing $2 billion a day and pledging the assets of we the American people as collateral.

Yes, folks, deficits do matter and the only difference between increased taxes and interest payments on our national debt is that the tax increases are the small part of the economic puzzle which we Americans are concerned with.

23

PUBLISHED JAN. 24, 2008

GETTING BACK TO A TRUE ECONOMY

For years now I have been writing letters and political columns stating that our U.S. economy was a false economy. It was and still is an economy propelled by consumer deficit spending and our federal government's deficit spending. It was and still is an economy which is unsustainable. Unsustainable means it cannot continue forever. Forever is here.

It's been said consumer spending is two-thirds of the U.S. economy. With two-thirds of the American consumers in debt or living paycheck to paycheck, and with a recession here or coming soon, consumer deficit spending is not going to bail out the economy. Neither is the U.S. deficit spending going to bail out the economy.

There is an old saying in business that "growth without profits is false growth." That's what we have had in the U.S.; growth without a balanced budget is the same as growth without profits.

Some highly educated people with no common sense or business sense say unbridled globalism and free world trade is inevitable. Many Americans who demand FAIR TRADE and insist on our American sovereignty being first and foremost are called "protectionists." We Americans who insist on fair trade and want to control our own economic destiny are NOT PROTECTIONISTS. We are nationalists who want to maintain our slipping standard of living in the U.S. More and more Americans hold jobs that don't pay a living wage, and those who can't even get a job need to be subsidized by other American taxpayers. In essence, this can tip the balance from our U.S. capitalistic government to a socialist government.

We Americans did not vote for socialism; however, that's what we are getting. Too many Americans are now in need of taxpayers' help to maintain their standard of living.

That's why the monthly U.S. job reports are, first of all, bogus, and secondly, irrelevant. New jobs that do not pay enough to maintain their own standard of living are really liabilities to our economy, and not assets.

America must enforce a fair trade policy, which will stop the flow of good paying American jobs from leaving the American economy. We can no longer let big business make products at the LOWEST worldwide costs and sell in America at the HIGHEST prices possible and pay America as little taxes as possible, as it lays off workers in the U.S. economy.

The housing crisis, the energy crisis, the U.S. consumer debt, the federal government deficit spending (our interest for 2007 exceeded $400 billion) and many other problems in the financial markets cannot be stopped from growing until we get fair trade and come to the realization that FREE TRADE is not FAIR TRADE.

There are those forecasters who are saying that the American economy will be in for a SOFT LANDING because of the strong world economy. I say for many middle income Americans who become poor it will be a depression, not a recession.

24

PUBLISHED JAN. 31, 2008

HOW TO FIX THE U.S. ECONOMY

First and foremost, we must get out of the WTO (World Trade Organization). It is an organization which is supposed to replace GATT, regulate world trade and lead us to global economic integration. It is yet another international bureaucracy whose functionaries will be largely autonomous.

The WTO reports to over 120 nations and therefore, in practice, to nobody. Each nation has one vote out of 120. Thus America will be handing over ultimate control of our economy to an unelected, uncontrolled group of international bureaucrats representing the best interests of large, multinational corporations.

Yes, the WTO is a WEALTH transfer organization, HEAVILY WEIGHTED against America, and the problem with free world trade is that ONLY AMERICA PRACTICES IT.

As it is written, the WTO laws can over-ride our American laws. How our President and Congress can go along with the WTO is beyond me. Could it be that big business money is keeping the U.S. Congress quiet about the WTO, or are they that dumb?

In either case, we must get out of the WTO. It is not good for our economy. It also threatens our national sovereignty and takes away our power to control our own economic destiny.

The second thing America must do to fix our economy is to declare our insolvency. In personal terms, we must declare our insolvency to protect our assets, which mainly is our $14 trillion economy.

America owes over $6 trillion, mostly to foreign countries, and about $3 trillion to our Social Security surplus. America paid $327 billion in interest on our debt as of Sept. 30th in fiscal year 2005, $406 billion in interest on our debt in the 2006 fiscal year, and nearly $500 billion on our debt in interest in the fiscal year 2007.

President Bush's deficits don't matter; economic policies since he was elected in 2000 have literally bankrupted the U.S. If deficits didn't matter, how come the interest on our debt went up from $327 billion to $406 billion, to $500 billion?

What America must do is freeze our U.S. Treasury bonds and only allow 10 percent to be withdrawn per year. Naturally, U.S. bond holders will get interest on the frozen bonds they own.

Japan, China, South Korea, some oil rich mid-east countries, etc., etc., have U.S. Treasury notes payable on demand. So, in essence, the foreign countries who hold U.S. Treasury notes can push the U.S. into bankruptcy. Of course, they don't want to do this because they will be killing the U.S. economy, which they so much depend upon.

Foreign countries have a minimum of $5 trillion which they can invest in America. We must make sure these investments do not threaten our national security or monopolize our economy.

The U.S. dollars that foreign countries have to invest in America are not the immediate problem facing America. The immediate problem is that America cannot provide the liquidity needed to China or any other country who wants to cash in their U.S. Treasury notes.

China has devalued their currency by about 40 percent, which allows them to drain billions of dollars from America with their trade imbalance with the U.S., plus the interest we pay them on our national debt. China has about a trillion in cash to invest in America or world-wide. However, it is the $450 billion U.S. Treasury notes which they hold over our head when we try to bargain for fair trade with them.

In order to get FAIR WORLD TRADE, which will provide the good jobs we need in our American economy, we must freeze our treasury notes and balance the American budget while paying down on our national debt.

China and every other foreign country still needs America's $14 trillion economy as much as we need them. We must put a 40 percent tariff on all Chinese imports until they stop devaluing their currency by 40 percent.

There are a lot of other things America must do to receive fair trade in the world-wide marketplace; however, freezing our treasury notes is the first big step.

The first argument the millions of intellectuals we have in America will say is the 40 percent tariff on Chinese imports will be highly inflationary.

If I am one of the millions of Americans who can't afford to put food on the table, put gas in the car, or heat their home in the winter and pay their taxes, I don't care if Chinese imports go up.

It is my opinion that when we put this 40 percent tariff on Chinese imports they will stop devaluing their currency by 40 percent. We have got to start playing hardball with China if we are going to break the stranglehold they have on our economy.

25

PUBLISHED SEPT. 17, 2007

ANTICIPATED INCOME

The first thing a family, city, state or federal government must do in preparing a budget for the following year is to come up with a dollar and sense figure to base their spending on.

This figure is called "anticipated income." Believe me, it's going to be revenue shortfalls that are going to be the biggest budget buster in the current session.

No, not excessive spending but revenue shortfall of the anticipated income is going to be the biggest problem for family, city, state and federal governments.

Countrywide Mortgage, the third largest lender (behind Fannie Mae and Freddie Mac) this Friday (Sept. 7) announced a 12,000 job layoff. This brings job loss to the mortgage industry to over 50,000.

Unlike some greedy stockholders who say Countrywide is cutting expenses (firing 12,000), I think I'll buy that stock because they will be turning a profit the next quarter or the next year. I grieve for the 12,000 families who lost good jobs that they cannot replace. I would dare say two-thirds of those 12,000 will have to accept jobs which pay less and with fewer, if any, benefits.

The millions of Americans who will lose good jobs in 2008 are going to be the reason city, state and federal governments are going to experience major revenue shortfalls on their anticipated income.

It's past time the president (oh, forget him) and the U.S. Congress start demanding fair trade agreements; pass new tax reform, which will make large corporations pay their fair share of taxes; cancel all NAFTA agreements, which are taking away American jobs in construction, manufacturing, hotel industry, trucking, etc.; then temporarily halt all H1 Visas, which are taking away American jobs, etc.

Am I a protectionist? No. I just want fair trade, which is in the best interests of America and not the large worldwide corporations.

I call myself an American who wants reciprocal trade agreements. If you must call me and others "protectionists," I say go ahead; pretty soon we will have nothing to protect.

26

PUBLISHED DEC. 27, 2007

WE MUST ACT NOW ON THE HOUSING CRISIS

In about a year, we will have a new president who will take office with the economy in a full blown recession.

We the American people and our U.S. Congress must act now to lessen the blow this recession will do to our economy.

First of all, our Congressmen and Senators must come out of their sandboxes, put their committee and subcommittee duties on the back burner and go to work on the housing problem, which is the main reason pushing our economy into a recession.

The first thing they must realize is that within a year or two many good, up-to-date prime mortgages will be in jeopardy of foreclosure because they (due to lower house valuations) do not have enough equity in their home mortgages.

This U.S. Congress must pass a bill as soon as possible which will not let lenders demand $10,000, $20,000, $30,000, $50,000 or more on their mortgages or face foreclosures.

Homeowners who have made their home mortgage payment on time should not have foreclosure hanging over their heads because their house has lost market value equity.

After the U.S. Congress passes this bill protecting U.S. homeowners from foreclosure, their next task is to become real estate agents and pass bills to help sell the supply of condos and houses on the market.

Whether it is going overseas to Japan, China, European countries, etc., and offering foreign citizens a H.O. Visa (Home Owners) if they buy a home in America, or also have the government offer interest free down payment loans, which are needed in today's market to buy a home. There has to be programs to help prospective homebuyers, like the college loan programs.

It is imperative for the U.S. Congress and we the American people to start selling homes now before the glut of homes in the U.S. housing industry causes the full blown recession due in early 2009. In 2008 we must sell, sell, sell condos and houses in the U.S. or face a recession, which will be a depression for many of us Americans.

Happy New Year. What we do to start moving condos and houses will be the barometer of working out of a recession or being in a bad recession in 2009, 2010, 2011, etc.

If the federal government and the real estate industry could convince many homeowners who own their own homes outright or have a small mortgage to reduce the price of the home they want to sell by $30,000 to $50,000, we could sell two houses instead of one.

There are many current homeowners who want to buy a new house, but they have to sell their house first. If we could get them to lower their price substantially they could sell their existing home (it will be worth less in a year or two anyway) and the house they want now is priced right or can be negotiated downward.

So if a current homeowner who wants a new home sells theirs, now we have taken two homes off the market.

27

PUBLISHED DEC. 13, 2007

U.S. GOVERNMENT WRONG AGAIN

Mortgage meltdown

The meltdown of the subprime mortgage market was as predictable as the morning sunrise or the swallows' return to San Juan Capistrano. Borrowers' financial ignorance, combined with lender greed, has undermined both our financial institutions and the real estate economy.

An unholy alliance of predatory lenders and unethical realtors and appraisers has led to phony appraisals and doctored loan applications. It has devastated the financial lives of many borrowers, it has defrauded financial and real estate investors, and it has jeopardized numerous businesses that service the real estate sector.

As Yogi Berra so aptly put it, "It' ain't over 'til it's over." The subprime meltdown will now reverberate through the prime real estate market. Home values will continue to flatten, and those homeowners who are facing fat loan balloons, or have used their home equity as their personal cash cow, will stare into the abyss. This is more than a few rotten apples. It is systemic fraud.

For our U.S. government, trying to sort out the subprime mortgages, it is another case of closing the barn door after the cows are gone. This bureaucratic plan of helping a few subprime borrowers keep their homes is not the answer to the housing crisis which will push the U.S. economy into a full blown recession in 2008.

What needs to be done as soon as possible is for the U.S. government and private think tanks to come up with innovative ways which will make it possible for prospective home buyers to buy a condo or house in today's market.

Unless we come up with ways to start moving nearly a year's supply of houses on the market today we cannot get a bottoming out price on homes. More importantly, we cannot start building the new houses needed to provide jobs for our economy.

I have submitted a couple of ideas to help prospective home buyers in today's market. One would be for our government to offer foreign citizens a H.O. (Home Owners) Permanent Visa if they buy a new home in America over $100,000. This incentive of a permanent Visa in America could attract foreigners with money to buy homes in America.

Also allow a husband and wife applying for a mortgage to include their working teenagers' wages in their income. Of course, the teenagers would be responsible, along with their parents, to pay off the mortgage.

I am sure many other Americans can think of innovative ways to help borrowers buy houses in today's market.

We must start selling houses and condos if we want to fix this housing crisis. If home prices keep going down, not only will subprime mortgages be a problem in 2008, but many prime mortgages will be in jeopardy as they will not have enough equity in their homes to avoid foreclosures.

28

PUBLISHED JULY 26, 2007

IT AIN'T OVER 'TIL IT'S OVER

In the past few years I have written several letters to the editor in regards to the ever-rising prices of homes (new and old). They were very over-valued and I couldn't see how middle income families could afford the mortgage payments and NH's highest-in-the-nation property taxes.

I was especially concerned about the new homeowners in NH who not only carried a $200,000 or $300,000 mortgage and still pay NH property taxes on their over-valued and over-appraised home. I knew that what goes up must come down, and the so-called mortgage meltdown is only the tip of the iceberg.

Mortgage meltdown

The meltdown of the subprime mortgage market was as predictable as the morning sunrise or the swallows' return to San Juan Capistrano. Borrowers' financial ignorance, combined with lender greed, has undermined both our financial institutions and the real estate economy.

An unholy alliance of predatory lenders and unethical realtors and appraisers has led to phony appraisals and doctored loan applications. It has devastated the financial lives of many borrowers, it has defrauded financial and real estate investors, and it has jeopardized numerous businesses that service the real estate sector.

As Yogi Berra so aptly put it, "It ain't over 'til it's over." The subprime meltdown will now reverberate through the prime real estate market. Home values will continue to flatten, and those homeowners who are facing fat loan balloons, or have used their home equity as their personal cash cow, will stare into the abyss. This is more than a few rotten apples. It is systemic fraud.

When will it hit bottom and what will the bottom be? A well known economist predicted 2009 and home values 30 percent less than today's home prices.

If he is correct, a $450,000 home today will be $315,000; a $300,000 home will be $210,000; a $200,000 home will be $140,000; and a $100,000 starter home or condo would be $70,000. This bottom of the mortgage meltdown will be in the next two years.

Yes, 2009 is right around the corner, and I have two suggestions for NH homeowners. Write your NH Congressman and Governor and tell them, "I am fighting foreclosure on my home and NH should start doing the math, substituting the NH property tax for an 8 percent sales tax." This 8 percent sales tax will equal the 8 percent room and meals tax we already have.

A personal friend of mine said, "Well, if property values go down, we NH homeowners will pay less taxes." NOT SO, whereas in NH we have no income or sales tax, if our property values go down they will just raise the tax evaluation.

So if your NH property tax evaluation goes down, your tax rate will go up.

The second piece of advice I have is if you're selling your house now, lower the asking price and accept any reasonable offer from an interested, qualified buyer. Your house will be worth 30 percent less in two years.

Also, if you have a house with three or four bedrooms and several baths, look for a person to rent a room and bath from you. Because if a husband and wife get divorced, or have huge hospital bills, or one loses their job, chances are you will get backed up financially and face foreclosure.

Last but not least, when the housing prices hit bottom, many homeowners will not have enough equity in their mortgage because their $300,000 home is now worth $210,000. Believe it or not, lenders can issue foreclosures to homeowners who have not missed a mortgage payment. They simply say "because of property devaluations we must have $20,000, $30,000 or $50,000 more on your mortgage or we will foreclose."

We should write our U.S. Congressman today and have them pass a law which will not let the lenders foreclose on any up-to-date loans because the home is worth less due to the real estate market. The way our U.S. Congress moves, we need to act now.

29

PUBLISHED SEPT. 27, 2007

FIRST WE MUST STOP THE BLEEDING

I have no medical background; however, I do know if a badly wounded person is brought into the Emergency Room they must first stop the bleeding.

In regards to foreclosures, pre-foreclosures, and future foreclosures, we must stabilize the housing market so that we, the American people, believe that the prices of homes have bottomed out and that houses and condos are selling 30 to 60 days upon going on the market for sale.

This would stop the bleeding in the housing market, which threatens to throw our economy into a recession.

No sense dwelling on the past sub-prime mortgage, loss of good jobs it takes to make mortgage payments, or the down payment and higher interest rates it now takes to buy a home. What we need are some innovative new policies to get houses moving again.

I propose a new H.O. (Home Owner) Visa. This H.O. Visa would give every Chinese, Japanese, European country, South Korean, etc., a permanent Visa to live in America if they purchase a house valued at $150,000 to $1 million. This Visa would be valid as long as they keep the house or re-sell it and buy another house.

I have read that there are over 30,000 Chinese who are, by American standards, millionaires. We welcome them to be homeowners in America as long as they pay their taxes and obey the laws in America. Did you know 70 percent of the Chinese are now learning to speak English?

I guess I would swap a Chinese nationalist with money who is learning English for a Mexican with no money who doesn't even want to learn English. That's a no-brainer.

Besides giving foreigners a H.O. Visa, we must make buying a home in America more than the conventional husband and wife or single ownership.

If a family applies for a mortgage with teenage kids, put their names on the mortgage as well as the parents. I am sure that if teenagers realize they, along with their parents, have the liability to pay off the mortgage that they will think about keeping the mortgage up to date before they want their own "wheels" or their own apartment or even putting college back a few years.

My grandfather bought a house in Massachusetts in 1920. He had seven children, and my mother was a fancy stitcher in the shoe factory, making $29 a week. He gave her $9 and kept the $20. Needless to say, he paid off this small mortgage and bought two big rides in an amusement park.

I am not saying we must confiscate the earnings of today's teenagers; HOWEVER, in today's housing market they must pay their share of the mortgage.

How about adding your or his father or mother as to a new home ownership with little or no down payment?

There must be many more innovative ways to help American families to buy a new home. The demand for new homes is out there. We just have to help prospective buyers to purchase and maintain these homes without causing another sub-prime mortgage debacle, which we still have to deal with.

Let's get houses selling again and stop the bleeding in the housing industry.

Remember, a house is a house until a family lives there, then it is a home. To lose your home, be it a trailer or a mansion, is a terrible experience and to also lose the equity in your home is a double tragedy!

30

PUBLISHED JULY 12, 2007

WE MUST ABOLISH THE IRS

Why is it that easy, common sense solutions to America's greatest economic and military problems can't be implemented to solve our growing problems before they become crises?

I believe the large world-wide corporations are controlling our government, looking out for their best interests and not the best interests of America.

I have just read (twice) the #1 best seller *The Fair Tax Book,* saying goodbye to the income tax and the IRS. This book advocates a nationwide consumption tax of about 23 percent. No other federal taxes.

By replacing the income tax with a consumption tax we, the American people, take back our government from the large world-wide corporations who are bypassing our Congress to foster their world-wide interests.

What are their world-wide interests? To manufacture goods at the lowest world-wide workforce wages and sell in America at the highest prices possible. Also, they want to drive down the wages in America while paying as little taxes as possible to our American government.

So what would abolishing the IRS and all other federal taxes do for America and we the American people? Well, for starters it would not eliminate our trade deficit; HOWEVER, it would make large world-wide corporations pay a 23 percent consumption tax, which really amounts to a 23 percent tariff on all goods sold in America. The world-wide corporations could continue making products with low (slave labor) costs in some cases and still sell in America at the highest prices they can get.

Make no mistake about it, this consumption tax would put sand in the gears of the world-wide corporations who are running our government.

Another major problem the fair tax would eliminate is America's ever-growing underground economy. More and more Americans and illegals are working under the table for cash and not paying the IRS one penny. Since we can't stop drugs in America at least the 23 percent consumption tax will make the drug dealers pay taxes when they buy goods and services with their drug money.

The knock against a consumption tax is that it will hurt poor and lower income Americans the most as they pay little or no income tax but would still have to pay a 23 percent nation-wide consumption tax. This is not true. Whereas the poor and lower income people are relieved of all federal taxes they still get Social Security and Medicaid. They also can work lower income jobs that could build up their family income.

Doesn't it make common sense that Americans who make the most money will pay the most consumption taxes?

I ask anyone who has read this guest commentary so far to go out and buy *The Fair Tax Book* written by talk show host Neal Boortz and Congressman John Linder. There is a national movement on this consumption tax replacing the IRS, so if you believe it's a fairer way to tax us Americans, I suggest you join the movement.

Do you know why the big businesses (Bush controlled) do not want to secure our borders with Mexico? Quite simply, they are, as we speak, bypassing our U.S. Congress to implement a North American free trade agreement with Mexico and Canada. They want to drive tractor trailers from the tip of Mexico through America onto the farthest point in Canada.

With this North American (free trade) agreement, the large world-wide corporations can avoid paying most all taxes and use the huge Mexican workforce to drive down the wages and benefits of the American workers.

If none of the presidential candidates running around every corner of NH will support a no IRS tax bill I will throw down $1,000 and have my name on the NH Primary for President of the United States to try to put the Fair Tax Bill into law, or at the very least, make it a national presidential issue.

31

PUBLISHED OCT. 18, 2007

THE FAIR TAX MOVEMENT

There is a growing movement in America to replace the IRS and all other federal taxes with a 23 percent federal sales tax. This consumption tax is called the Fair Tax and is explained from A to Z in Neal Boortz and John Linder's best-selling book, *The Fair Tax Book*.

In my opinion, the 23 percent federal sales tax (consumption tax) is the only way to get the large corporations (American in name only) to pay their fair share of taxes to the U.S. government.

As it is now, these large multi-national corporations are investing in Third World countries like Vietnam, where they work for much less than $1 an hour. This manufactured product made in Vietnam is shipped to America and sold for the highest price possible. The final result is (like trade with China) Americans losing good jobs in our country.

Now I ask anybody: How can America compete with slave wages like that? The answer is that we can't. So as America loses more good jobs each year from "free world trade," the American government receives LESS federal taxes as the large corporations in America lay off workers with good jobs year after year.

In the last Republican debate, Fred Thompson was asked about the state of the American economy. Fred said, "The American economy is strong and is experiencing 22 quarters of increased GDP (Gross Domestic Product)" etc., etc.

I have a follow-up question for Fred. How come in the last 22 quarters (nearly six years) the federal deficit has risen from $4.8 trillion to over $9 trillion?

The answer is that America has a false economy buoyed by federal deficit spending and consumer deficit spending. It is an unsustainable economy which will not have a soft landing when the bubble bursts.

The IRS is not providing the money the U.S. government needs to balance their budget. The Fair Tax has a name which implies that we are swapping the IRS for the Fair Tax because it is fair to the American people. This is not the reason. The reason is that the IRS, in this era of unbridled globalism, is not getting enough taxes to supply the American government with their fair share of taxes in the global marketplace.

With the new consumption tax (called Fair Tax), the U.S. will get 23 percent of all goods sold in America regardless of if they are made in China or Vietnam.

Also, the Fair Tax will make all the underground economy (which is billions and billions) pay their taxes (which they currently don't pay a penny of) and the people profiting from the sale of drugs will also pay taxes when they purchase their new home or Mercedes automobile.

Yes, getting rid of the IRS for a 23 percent consumption tax is the number one issue in 2008. If our government doesn't have the money it needs, how can the U.S. government continue to operate without experiencing a financial crisis?

So I cannot support any candidate for president in either party (or possibly third party) who does not want to get rid of the IRS for a 23 percent consumption tax (Fair Tax).

32

PUBLISHED DEC. 6, 2007

GOVERNOR HUCKABEE COULD WIN THE REPUBLICAN NOMINATION

The first thing he has to do is call a spade a spade, having called for all federal taxes (including the IRS) to be abolished in favor of a new Fair Tax.

He must become a salesman and sell this new federal consumption tax to the American people. The very name "The Fair Tax" is working against him. He should refer to the new tax replacing the IRS as a national sales tax and not a fair tax.

By calling the national sales tax a fair tax it opens up a can of worms as to whether this new tax is fair to all Americans. Well we all know life is not fair, and Americans will holler when some tax is unfair to them but say nothing when taxes are unfair to others.

This so called fair tax is not about getting rid of the IRS because of fairness. This new national sales tax is a consumption tax, which will bring in billions and billions of dollars into the U.S. Treasury. It is instrumental in leveling the playing field in today's unfair trading practices.

Let me explain. When America trades with Japan, the European community, South Korea and maybe a few other countries we have the same wage scales, employee benefits, and environmental rules so this is fair trade, which America, with its great productivity, can compete with. The problem is that America opens its market to free world trade while these other countries do not. We can take care of this unfairness if we have the will to do so.

Why we need the consumption tax is to level the playing field with China, Vietnam and other nations who pay their workers $1 to $2 per hour. How is America, even with our great productivity and competitiveness, going to compete with slave labor wages?

As I am writing this letter, China has a 25 percent tariff on American automobiles sold in China. At the same time they, with Chrysler's help, are building a joint automobile factory in Mexico. These cars will sell for

$9,000 to $10,000 and they, with their cash, can offer U.S. consumers no down payment deals.

This is going to cause great job layoffs to the American auto industry. These laid off workers have good jobs with which they pay high taxes, purchase most goods and services, plus they don't need any government or taxpayers' money to subsidize their standard of living.

If we had the new consumption tax, America would collect 23 percent of all the new cars made in Mexico and financed by China.

So the new tax (Note: I didn't say fair tax) will level the playing field in America's favor when trying to trade with countries who pay slave labor wages. This new tax will increase the revenues going into the U.S. Treasury.

Another thing the consumption tax will do is tax the underground economy who, as of now, pay no federal IRS taxes.

Illegals and many other Americans who receive cash for their goods and services do not report this income. This growing underground economy could easily amount to $500 billion a year.

Also, the drug dealers in America now pay no taxes. Under the new consumption tax they will pay taxes when they spend that illegal money.

So in my opinion, the new federal sales tax or consumption tax will put billions into the U.S. Treasury.

If Republican (second tier) candidate for president Governor Huckabee (as the polls show he may take the Iowa caucus), he would only have to come in second or third with a high NH vote to have the momentum going into South Carolina and that all-important Feb. 5 national primary.

I hope Gov. Huckabee sticks to his guns and pursues this major issue of replacing the IRS with a national sales tax.

33

PUBLISHED DEC. 13, 2007

AS SHAKESPEARE SAID, "WHAT'S IN A NAME?"

"A rose by any other name would smell as sweet ..." etc., etc., etc.

The "Fair Tax" which Governor Huckabee called for to replace the IRS, is a CONSUMPTION tax. To me it is irrelevant if some Americans (especially the large American-in-name-only corporations) say the "Fair Tax" is unfair.

The Fair Tax Book: Saying Goodbye to the Income Tax and the IRS, a comprehensive book on the "Fair Tax" system written by Neil Boortz and Congressman John Linder, should be renamed. How about just simply calling it a consumption tax and dropping the argumentative name of a "Fair Tax"? Let's call the Fair Tax a woman who is getting married and changing her last name.

The consumption tax, or federal sales tax, if you must, is needed to replace the IRS because it will bring billions and billions of dollars into the U.S. Treasury. It will make Big Business pay their fair share into the U.S. Treasury.

The large, multi-national U.S. corporations will spend billions of dollars in Congress to defeat the new consumption tax, which will replace the IRS.

That's why I, as an undeclared registered voter in NH, am leaning toward the possibility of voting for Governor Huckabee in the Republican presidential primaries. At least I know that Big Business has not, as of yet, bought out the Governor who speaks the truth.

What the "Fair Tax" or consumption tax will do for America:

- Eliminate the income tax and the dreaded IRS

- Jump-start the U.S. economy

- Bring businesses and jobs back to the United States

- Recapture billions of untaxed dollars currently lost to criminal and offshore businesses

What the "Fair Tax" or consumption tax will do for you:

- Allow you to keep 100 percent of your hard-earned paycheck

- Let you choose to save all the money you want ... and pay taxes only when you spend it

- Eliminate countless taxes you don't even know you're paying

- Make April 15 just another beautiful spring day

I thought I listed all of my opposition to the IRS in my last political column; however, I missed one big point – that being tens of thousands of U.S. citizens are not even filing their income tax returns.

What's the IRS doing to get these tax evaders? The answer is nothing.

However, as a life-long businessman who has paid hundreds of thousands in federal income taxes and has been audited three times, I didn't have to pay any more income to the IRS three times.

No, the IRS is not fair when they don't go after those who don't file income tax returns but audit those who do.

Another reason the IRS should be eliminated in favor of a consumption tax is that we must not let Big Business continue their mission, which is to manufacture goods anywhere in the world at the LOWEST COST possible, to sell anywhere in the world (mostly in America) at the HIGHEST PRICES POSSIBLE, and to pay as little taxes as possible to the U.S. Treasury.

The "Fair Tax," I mean the consumption tax, makes Big Business pay 23 percent to the U.S. Treasury whether it is made in Vietnam or any other slave wages nation who pays their employees $1 or $2 per hour.

How they (large multinational corporations) are now trying to pull the wool over on the American public: On TV, I saw a modern, air-conditioned factory in Vietnam which was filled with women 20 years old or older, all in nice uniforms, working in the factory. They, Big Business, wanted to give the impression to us Americans that their new factories in Vietnam were not SWEAT SHOPS and their employees were not child labor.

The next day I read in the newspaper that the average wage of Vietnamese textile workers was $120 to $150 a MONTH. That was it. No hourly wage or weekly hours worked. They didn't ever say this $120 to $150 monthly wage was net income or gross income. It is my guess that these Vietnamese workers have to pay the Vietnamese government some taxes out of their monthly income.

Just think of it. If they (the Vietnamese workers) were getting $1 an hour for 40 hours that would only give them $40 a week, which is $160 a month. My guess is they get much less than $1 per hour and their work week is much more than 40 hours a week.

Big Business may want to give the impression that they do not run sweat shops or hire child labor. However, it is still SLAVE LABOR, which America cannot compete with.

We must have the consumption tax to replace the IRS to level the playing field when the U.S. trades with countries that have a slave labor workforce.

34

PUBLISHED DEC. 18, 2007

MY PRIMARY VOTE IS VERY IMPORTANT TO ME

President Bush, before he leaves office, will set the Republican Party back about 100 years. Would I vote for a Republican in the NH primaries, and would I vote for a Republican in the general election? The answer is yes.

As much as I blame President Bush and the Republican Party for the handling of the Iraq War and the path they have led to the U.S. heading to a world financial crisis in which we, the American people, will be the big losers.

On Oct. 12, I went down to the Barrington Town Hall and changed my party affiliation from Democrat to Undeclared. I did this after much thought and deliberation. As much as I detested the nearly two terms of Bush's Republican Party policies, I couldn't shut the door on any Republican candidate for president who best represented my nationalistic views.

As an UNDECLARED (Independent), I can ask for a Democratic or Republican ballot in the Jan. 8 NH primaries. I am going to ask for a Republican ballot and vote for Gov. Mike Huckabee.

Gov. Huckabee wants to replace the IRS and other federal taxes with a consumption tax, now misnamed the Fair Tax. Unbridled globalism, if allowed to continue, will push America's lower-income and middle-income citizens (and yes, a few higher income Americans) into the poor class.

Large worldwide corporations want to manufacture goods at the lowest possible costs, sell these manufactured products worldwide (primarily in America) at the highest prices possible and pay America and other countries as little taxes as possible.

America cannot compete in the world market with countries like China and Vietnam who employ slave labor. We need the consumption tax (aka Fair Tax) to level the playing field. Under the consumption tax, the U.S. Treasury will get 23 percent of all slave labor manufactured goods sold in America.

Since we have made peace with Communist Vietnam, American corporations have invested billions into their economy to tap in on their slave labor workforce.

Isn't that something – the U.S. government sends hundreds of thousands of U.S. military to give their life fighting the no-end/no-win war against Communist Vietnam, now big business is investing in Communist Vietnam to take away jobs from many Americans who fought Communism in Vietnam.

We need a revolution in America against trade with slave labor nations. China should be on the top of the list, and a consumption tax is a must.

35

PUBLISHED OCT. 4, 2007

THE IRANIAN PEOPLE MUST STOP THEIR MADMAN PRESIDENT BEFORE IT'S TOO LATE

America does not have to worry about Iran building nuclear weapons. Israel will not let that happen. With their intelligence, Israel will bomb any Iranian nuclear facility whenever they feel it's necessary. Why wouldn't they? Do you honestly believe Israel will let Iran develop nuclear weapons, which Iran will use to destroy Israel?

After Israel destroys all of Iran's nuclear facilities, will Iran start a full-scale war against Israel? Hell no, they fear Israel's military power! They will cry to the UN and other world powers.

Israel has its borders secure and they retaliate after every act of terrorism. Besides their battle proven military, Israel has a nuclear arsenal as a deterrent to any other country who would even think of destroying Israel.

One must remember – Islamic fanatics, with their uncivil acts of violence against innocent men, women and children, are cowards who run away from conventional war on the battlefield.

Just look at their six-day war against Israel 20-some years ago; just look how they ran away from battle in Desert Storm; look how they ran away from America's forces when we took Saddam Hussein out of power in Baghdad. Islamic militants only know terrorist war, they will not fight on the battlefield.

Why do you think Israel has survived all these years?

1. They have their borders secure.

2. They retaliate for every terrorist act upon their country.

3. They have a military super power ready to spring into action.

4. And last, but not least, they have nuclear weapons as a deterrent.

So to America I say: Don't worry about Iran having nuclear weapons, Israel will not let that happen.

Also, I want to warn the Iranian people: Be careful what your crazy, loudmouth Iranian president is wishing for – he just might get it.

The Iranian people must realize that pursuing nuclear weapons will bring total destruction to Iran. Forget nuclear weapons.

36

PUBLISHED OCT. 24, 2007

IT'S A WHOLE NEW BALL GAME

Several weeks ago in one of my letters to the editor I stated that America would not have to worry about Iran getting nuclear weapons because Israel would not let them progress that far in their nuclear program.

Israel, to protect their own existence, would bomb all Iranian nuclear facilities before Iran could produce nuclear weapons.

I also said that the terrorist community of Iran would not retaliate against Israel on the battlefield because they are cowards who only know uncivil terrorist tactics.

I also said that Iran would go to the United Nations and other powerful countries for help against Israel's bombing their nuclear facilities in Iran.

RUSSIA TO THE RESCUE

Iran, with their oil, money and trade, has got Russian President Putin to publicly back Iran's right to build a nuclear program for a domestic energy supply.

This Russian commitment throws sand in the gears of any U.S. or U.N. sanctions on Iran in an effort for Iran to not go ahead with their nuclear program.

I think that Russia's siding with Iran starts a whole new ball game. Iran will step to the plate and begin building their PEACEFUL nuclear program.

Will Russia's siding with Iran stop Israel from taking out Iran's nuclear facilities? The answer is no. However, the timing of Israel's attack on Iran will probably be SOONER rather than LATER. The ball game is on, and Israel will not sit and wait for a SECOND HOLOCAUST.

For those of us Americans who were thinking the Cold War with Russia was over, we had better think again.

37

PUBLISHED OCT. 29, 2007

AMERICA COULD LEAVE IRAQ WITH OUR HEADS HELD HIGH IF WE PLAY OUR CARDS RIGHT

IRAN

The President of Iran, Mahmoud Ahmadinejad, several years ago publicly denied the Holocaust promised to destroy Israel and America.

Since then, Iran has supplied terrorists with money, weapons, missiles, and roadside bombs to be used against America and Israel. They have let up on Israel after their failed missile assault launched from Syria a year or so ago.

Make no mistake about it; Iran fears retaliatory reactions from Israel, that's why they are holding back terrorist acts on Israel.

However, Iran, with Russia's backing, is pursuing nuclear weapons to destroy Israel. They simply will give terrorist groups the nuclear weapons to destroy Israel.

Iran, as of now, does not fear an attack on them from the United States because they know the U.S. Congress and the American people will not let this happen.

ISRAEL

Israel will not let Iran proceed with their plans for nuclear weapons. They, sooner or later, will have to launch all-out air strikes against Iran's nuclear facilities and military installations.

The Israeli people – whose mothers, fathers, grandparents, aunts and uncles, nieces and nephews, and friends were murdered in the first Holocaust – will not let a second Holocaust happen in their lifetime.

The fact that Iran has publicly announced the destruction of Israel and is hell-bent on securing nuclear weapons, plus the latest announcement by Iran that it has 11,000 missiles to be launched if Israel attacks them, is provocation enough for Israel to proceed with the inevitable war with Iran.

AMERICA

America must let Israel attack Iran alone. This cannot be a dual attack on Iran by Israel and America.

Now as soon as Israel's planes bomb Iran, Iran will launch some, or as many as possible, missiles at Israel.

If Iran sends any of these 11,000 missiles to American forces in Iraq, to any American war ships or American bases in the Middle East, then we can retaliate with our superior Air Force and Naval superiority and a real war will begin and end shortly.

The American Congress and the American people will not let Iran rain missiles down on Americans without full retaliation.

THE AFTERMATH

Once Israel and America have literally destroyed all of Iran's military capabilities, we can leave Iraq. The Iraqis don't want us there. They even said a few weeks ago that they don't even want U.S. bases in Iraq.

Yes, after we take care of Iran we can all come home and say mission accomplished!

The civil and religious battles in the Middle East will continue, with a group declaring itself the winner. However, Iran will not be able to pick up all the pieces and Iran's President, Mahmoud Ahmadinejad, is not going down in history as the Hitler of the Middle East who started World War III.

38

PUBLISHED NOV. 6, 2007

ISRAEL MUST LAUNCH ALL OUT AIR STRIKES AGAINST IRAN AS SOON AS POSSIBLE

Israelis realize that an all-out war with Iran is inevitable. So the sooner they can strike the first offensive blow in the war, the safer Israel will be.

The Israeli Air Force can (with a massive attack) take out most all of Iran's military operations. Their intelligence has all of Iran's strategic locations as targets for Israel's Air Force to annihilate with a massive bombardment.

At the same time Israel is engaging in an all-out bombing of Iran, they should be enforcing the Israeli border with their tanks, artillery and infantry.

Israel must also enforce their anti-missile equipment and have their citizens prepare for a missile attack from Iran. Israel must, after their attack against Iran, still fight a retaliatory war against Iran. They cannot mount any military offense on the ground. After Iran suffers their defeat in the air attack, they will be in no position to mount a ground war with Israel.

Iran will cry to Russia and possibly China to help them engage the Israelis in war.

AMERICA

As soon as Israel attacks Iran, America must be ready for missiles showered on American installations from Iran.

That's the green light for America's superior Air Force to wipe up, or should I say mop up, whatever is left of Iran's military operations in Iran.

Iran will be so totally destroyed they will want to do more crying than fighting on the battlefield.

America can then leave Iraq (100%) and come home and say MISSION ACCOMPLISHED.

We have taken out Iraq's Saddam Hussein and Iranian President Mahmoud Ahmadinejad. So the world is a safer place even though we spilled much blood and money in the last four years in Iraq.

Money is money, but we must not spill any more American blood in Iraq's civil/religious war.

This column is my last PAID POLITICAL COLUMN. In my mind, these ARE POLITICAL COLUMNS, NOT POLITICAL ADVERTISEMENTS as this newspaper insists on calling them.

Some of my friends ask me why I spent so much money on my political convictions. I ask them if they saw the March cover of *Newsweek*, which showed a young American woman in Iraq with both her legs blown off. What's money?

39

PUBLISHED DEC. 18, 2003

THE WTO WINS ROUND ONE

PRESIDENT BUSH PUT THE WORLD ECONOMY BEFORE THE AMERICAN ECONOMY BY TAKING OFF U.S. STEEL TARIFFS 15 MONTHS BEFORE OUR U.S. LAW WOULD HAVE ENDED U.S. TARIFFS

Bowing to the WTO (World Trade Organization), who ruled our U.S. steel tariffs ILLEGAL, and bowing to the threat of a miniscule trade war, President Bush dealt a SEVERE BLOW to our AMERICAN STEEL INDUSTRY, which was JUST BEGINNING TO STABILIZE and ADD NEW MANUFACTURING JOBS TO OUR ECONOMY.

In March of 2002, the U.S. Congress PROVED that the foreign countries were DUMPING STEEL into the U.S. economy at prices way BELOW COST. The foreign countries subsidized their country's businesses so they could TAKE AWAY AMERICAN STEEL WORKERS' JOBS and BUILD UP their STEEL EXPORTS TO AMERICA. Which, of course, would provide GOOD PAYING MANUFACTURING JOBS FOR THEIR ECONOMY.

President Bush, in March of 2002, had NO ALTERNATIVE but to sign our three-year (36-month) steel tariff levied to SAVE OUR STEEL INDUSTRY from UNFAIR TRADE PRACTICES which threaten to put our U.S. steel industry OUT OF BUSINESS.

Before this March 2002 U.S. steel tariff law the U.S. had 31 STEEL COMPANIES GO BANKRUPT and MANY OTHER American steel companies NEAR BANKRUPTCY.

THE U.S. STEEL TARIFFS DID WORK

For the 21 months that we imposed our U.S. steel tariffs we have stabilized our steel industry, in fact our domestic steel industry is growing.

Wilbur Ross, now chairman of the U.S. steel industry, said on the CNN Lou Dobbs show that we must keep the U.S. steel tariffs the full 36 months and that much of the progress made in our steel industry can be negated by an early cancelling of our steel tariffs.

It was Wilbur Ross who, in a public speech last year, called the WTO a WEALTH TRANSFER ORGANIZATION WITH INTERESTS HEAVILY WEIGHTED

AGAINST THE UNITED STATES, AND THE TERRIBLE FLAW IN FREE WORLD TRADE IS THAT ONLY AMERICA PRACTICES IT.

I have written in many of my political ads that America CANNOT CONTROL ITS OWN ECONOMIC DESTINY WHEN WTO LAWS CAN MAKE OUR AMERICAN LAWS ILLEGAL.

I, JOHN DONALD RIGAZIO, REPUBLICAN PRESIDENTIAL CANDIDATE IN NH'S FIRST IN THE NATION PRESIDENTIAL PRIMARY, WILL DO TWO THINGS FOR OUR ECONOMY.

1. Establish a new homeland security for OUR ECONOMY which will PASS U.S. LAWS AND ENFORCE U.S. LAWS TO STABILIZE AND REBUILD OUR ECONOMY.

2. In order to do this, the United States of America must GET OUT OF THE WTO and we must tell our trading partners TRADE IS A TWO-WAY STREET.

MAYBE A LITTLE TRADE WAR WOULD HELP BRING DOWN OUR 500 BILLION TRADE DEFICIT IN 2003 WHICH, IF ALLOWED TO CONTINUE, WILL DESTROY OUR AMERICAN ECONOMY.

40

PUBLISHED NOV. 15, 2003

PRESIDENT BUSH MUST NOT TAKE OFF OUR STEEL TARIFFS, OR WE CAN KISS OUR STEEL INDUSTRY GOODBYE

In March of 2002 the United States placed tariffs on foreign steel from countries which had been DUMPING STEEL IN THE AMERICAN MARKETPLACE FOR BELOW THEIR COSTS.

In the past 10 years the United States had 30 STEEL COMPANIES GO BANKRUPT. This has been a CRIPPLING BLOW to THE MANUFACTURING SEGMENT of our economy.

The steel tariffs HAVE STABILIZED our steel industry and ADDED A NEW STEEL COMPANY which is made up of the former bankrupt company Bethlehem Steel and another defunct U.S. steel company. This new steel company has ADDED 18,000 NEW JOBS to our manufacturing base. Its new CEO, Wilbur Ross, is an OPEN CRITIC OF THE WTO.

So in July of 2002 the United States, WITHOUT TARIFFS, imported 298 million metric tons of foreign steel. In July 2003 the United States IMPORTED 198 metric tons of steel WITH THE U.S. TARIFFS. During this year (July 2002 to July 2003), our new steel company opened by Wilbur Ross MUST HAVE PRODUCED 100 MILLION METRIC TONS OF STEEL IN THE UNITED STATES.

The WTO (World Trade Organization), on JULY 12 of this year, RULED OUR UNITED STATES TARIFFS ILLEGAL. We naturally APPEALED and on NOV. 3 the WTO JUST RULED AGAINST OUR APPEAL and the United States has FIVE DAYS TO TAKE OFF OUR TARIFFS ON FOREIGN STEEL.

The European community, who has one vote for each country in the WTO, has 13 VOTES to the United States' ONE VOTE. They and other foreign countries have threatened us, the United States of America, with reciprocal trade tariffs on U.S. goods into the E.U. to the tune of 2.1 billion dollars. This is IF THE UNITED STATES DOES NOT take off our steel tariffs.

WHO IS THE WTO?

The WTO is an organization which is supposed to REGULATE INTERNATIONAL TRADE and LEAD US TO GLOBAL ECONOMIC INTEGRATION. It is just another international bureaucracy whose functionaries are LARGELY AUTONOMOUS. They report to over 120 nations and therefore in PRACTICE TO NOBODY. EACH NATION WILL HAVE ONE VOTE OUT OF 120. Thus, AMERICA and every European nation will be handing over ultimate control over its economy to an UNELECTED, UNCONTROLLED GROUP OF INTERNATIONAL BUREAUCRATS.

WILBUR R. ROSS SAYS

"The WTO is a WEALTH TRANSFER ORGANIZATION which is HEAVILY WEIGHTED AGAINST U.S. INTERESTS, and the FLAW IN FREE WORLD TRADE IS ONLY THE UNITED STATES PRACTICES IT."

I, John Donald Rigazio, say the United States CANNOT CONTROL OUR OWN ECONOMIC DESTINY WHILE A MEMBER OF THE WTO.

Only myself, a REPUBLICAN candidate for president, and Dennis J. Kucinich, a DEMOCRAT for president, want OUT OF THE WTO.

NOT ONLY DO I, JOHN DONALD RIGAZIO, WANT OUT OF THE WTO, I WANT A NEW HOMELAND SECURITY FOR OUR ECONOMY.

Here are just some of the SO-CALLED RADICAL measures that my new Department of Homeland Security for the economy should address.

1. Put the AMERICAN economy BEFORE the GLOBAL economy by withdrawing from international organizations that THREATEN OUR SOVEREIGNTY and ECONOMIC INDEPENDENCE.

2. BREAK OPEN foreign markets to American products with RECIPROCAL TRADE TREATIES.

3. Oppose fast track authority as a unilateral surrender by Congress of its constitutional power to amend trade treaties. THE PRESIDENT SHOULD NOT HAVE FAST TRACK TRADE AUTHORITY.

4. Resist expansion or extension of NAFTA and GATT.

5. Push for WITHDRAWAL FROM THE WTO and a return to BILATERAL TRADE TREATIES enforced by the U.S. and its trade partners.

6. Protect vital American industries by passing and enforcing TOUGH ANTI-DUMPING LEGISLATION.

7. Impose tariffs on foreign imports equal to the taxes imposed on goods made in the U.S. and use the revenue to cut American income taxes OR BALANCE THE FEDERAL BUDGET.

8. Etc., etc., etc.

THERE IS NO LIGHT AT THE END OF THE TUNNEL IN REGARDS TO OUR ECONOMY. CONTINUED JOB LOSSES AT HOME WILL, IN A FEW YEARS, DESTROY OUR STANDARD OF LIVING, BRING ON GREATER TAXATION, TAKE AWAY MORE OF OUR FREEDOMS AND CREATE CIVIL VIOLENCE IN MOST ALL AMERICAN CITIES.

41

PUBLISHED SEPT. 20, 2007

THE WTO (WORLD TRADE ORGANIZATION) IS A WEALTH TRANSFER ORGANIZATION

About five years ago, then millionaire (now billionaire) Wilbur E. Ross made a public statement that I haven't heard repeated since.

He said (and I still have the front page *USA Today* article), "The World Trade Organization is a Wealth Transfer Organization not in the BEST INTERESTS of America, and the PROBLEM with free world trade is that only America PRACTICES it."

When I ran for President of the U.S. in the 2004 Republican primary, my main issue was fair trade. So quite naturally I demanded that the U.S. get out of the WTO. In the 2004 primary, ONLY Democrat Dennis Kucinich WAS THEN and STILL IS today demanding the U.S. get out of the WTO.

WHAT IS WEALTH? AND HOW IS IT TRANSFERRED?

The wealth of a nation is all the workers who have good jobs. They pay the most taxes, purchase the most goods and services, and don't use any of the taxpayers' money to subsidize their standard of living.

That's the WEALTH of a nation. The more good jobs a country provides for its workers, the WEALTHIER the country becomes. Conversely, the more good jobs it loses, part of its WEALTH goes along with the job losses.

So that's how the WTO transfers WEALTH from America around the world with UNFAIR TRADE AGREEMENTS that do not benefit the United States of America but benefit the large world-wide corporations in their quest to buy as cheap as they can world-wide, to sell as high as they can world-wide, and to pay as little taxes as possible world-wide.

RIGAZIO FOR PRESIDENT 2004

Did I really have any political aspirations of becoming President of the U.S.? OF COURSE NOT. However, I was very serious about my solutions to the many problems in 2004 that have now become near crises.

I received a little more than 1,000 votes in the 2004 Republican primary election. Myself and two others got about 1,000 votes each and George W. got 53,000 votes.

I figured IF I could have gotten 5,000 or 6,000 votes the media would pay attention to my campaign issues. It didn't happen. I also figured the public who DISAPPROVED of George W. Bush's policies would have given me some protest votes; it didn't happen.

Well, what did it cost me? Besides the $1,000 fee to be on the NH ballot, I spent nearly $200,000 of my own money. I sent back five checks totaling $200 to someone who wanted to help my campaign. I had a first-class website and spent most of my money in newspaper ads in *Foster's* and *Manchester Union Leader.*

Knowing what I know now, would I still have run for President in the 2004 NH state primaries? HELL NO. For Americans to re-elect Bush shows how uninformed we are on national issues.

It's just poetic justice that Bush got re-elected so he can be in office when his war still divides the country and his federal deficits will cost us $400 billion a year in interest each and every year, and he leaves our economy in a very bad recession due to his economic policies.

God bless America and the new President of 2009 and the American people who will be paying for George W. Bush's eight years in office for years to come.

After reading this column, I would be less than honest if I didn't say what bothered me most about my running for President in 2004 was the people who viewed my candidacy as a big joke and didn't even read my positions on the issues.

And to my immediate family who felt I was embarrassing them: To this I tell them publicly, T.S.

42

PUBLISHED DEC. 6, 2003

THE UNITED STATES IS GOING TO HAVE A $500 BILLION TRADE DEFICIT THIS YEAR

Our President and other SO-CALLED FREE TRADERS want to ELIMINATE this trade deficit by EXPORTING MORE.

My COMMON SENSE tells me we CANNOT INCREASE OUR EXPORTS while trading with China, India, Mexico and a hundred other Third World nations whose people WORK FOR 1/10 OR 1/20 of the WAGES WE AMERICANS GET.

Also, the INDUSTRIAL NATIONS that do have almost equal wages of the U.S. workers are NOT OPENING THEIR MARKETS FULLY TO THE U.S., and they are SUBSIDIZING their countries' businesses to TAKE AWAY AMERICAN JOBS.

Yes, the industrial nations, namely the European community, Japan and South Korea, WORK WITH THEIR BUSINESSES TO TAKE JOBS AWAY FROM THE U.S. ECONOMY.

IF THE U.S. CAN'T EXPORT MORE, THEN WE MUST IMPORT LESS

The American economy, as I envision it, is like the TITANIC and UNLESS WE CHANGE ITS COURSE we will LOSE ALL OUR POKER CHIPS in a RIGGED GAME CALLED FREE WORLD TRADE.

It is ironic that the United States invited all the FOREIGN COUNTRIES TO THE TABLE in this poker game and GAVE THEM CHIPS TO PLAY THE GLOBAL POKER GAME.

NEXT YEAR, 2005, THE UNITED STATES MUST HAVE A ZERO FOREIGN TRADE DEFICIT

Most of us Americans know we have a nearly 7 trillion dollar national debt. Most of us INFORMED Americans also know our government has used over 3 TRILLION of Social Security surplus, which really should bring our 7 TRILLION national debt to over 10 TRILLION. I guess if the U.S. owes the 3 TRILLION TO THE SOCIAL SECURITY SYSTEM we, in reality, OWE IT TO OURSELVES so it ISN'T EVEN ACCOUNTED FOR.

To make our financial situation EVEN WORSE, President Bush's 2004 budget, which began Oct. 1 this year and ends Sept. 30, 2004, will produce a trillion-dollar deficit. The Bush Administration is already forecasting the 2004 budget deficit for 500 billion, that's not counting the Social Security surplus of about 300 billion they will spend every year and don't account for. That's 800 billion, plus 2004 REVENUE SHORTFALLS will push the TRUE 2004 BUSH BUDGET to a record 1 TRILLION DOLLAR DEFICIT.

HOW THE TRADE DEFICIT FOR 2005 IS THE KEY TO AMERICA'S TRUE ECONOMIC RECOVERY

Our current 2004 projected trade deficit NOT ONLY takes away GOOD AMERICAN JOBS from our own economy but it also LETS FOREIGN COUNTRIES BUY U.S. TREASURY BONDS TO FINANCE OUR TRADE DEFICITS.

The Japanese for years now have been buying U.S. Treasury bonds to finance our trade deficit with them.

Our trade deficit with China is estimated at 130 billion this year; China, as we speak, OWNS 120 BILLION IN U.S. TREASURY BONDS.

IF WE CONTINUE OUR CURRENT 500 BILLION TRADE DEFICITS THEN AMERICA WILL RUN OUT OF POKER CHIPS IN THE RIGGED WORLDWIDE POKER GAME

I say ELIMINATE the 2005 trade deficits to ZERO by IMPORTING LESS (THAT IS WITHIN OUR HANDS). EXPORTING MORE under the global trade laws enforced BY THE WTO IS IMPOSSIBLE.

The LONGER AMERICA WAITS to achieve our ZERO TRADE BALANCE the more Japan, China and others will AMASS BILLIONS OF U.S. TREASURY BONDS which they could CALL IN and put America and the world into a FINANCIAL CRISIS which could lead to WAR or in the VERY LEAST THREATS OF WAR.

43

PUBLISHED FEB. 7, 2008

THE TRUTH ABOUT SOCIAL SECURITY

In the early 1970s, the U.S. government came up with a good piece of legislation. Knowing that the Social Security Trust Fund would need much more money to pay out to the baby boomers, they made employers match the 6.2 percent withdrawn from their employees' paychecks on a weekly basis.

So for many years now the Social Security system has paid 12.4 percent each paycheck to the Social Security Trust Fund. When the employers had to match the employees' 6.2 percent payroll withholding tax, it doubled the money paid in to Social Security.

Add to this the decade of the '70s with 100 percent inflation rate wages, and Social Security payments to the U.S. government skyrocketed.

In 1983, the Republican administration transferred the Social Security Trust Fund into the general government revenues. Since 1983 (with the exception of the Democratic Clinton administration of 1992 to 2000) the federal government has been using the Social Security Trust Fund as a cash cow. They have taken over $3 trillion from the Social Security account.

The highly respected Concord Coalition speculates that Social Security will be in red ink by the year 2017. When that time comes, (sooner or later) the U.S. government can do a few minor adjustments to make sure the Social Security system is alive and well.

Social Security is one of the few government programs that pays for itself. It may have a slight cold in 2017 but it will need only a teaspoon of cough syrup to ensure its recovery.

However, it is the health care system entitlements which will bankrupt the U.S. Each year, health care costs in the U.S. go up about 10 percent more. It serves fewer and fewer Americans at higher and higher costs. Unlike Social Security, it is not funded by the 12.4 percent withholding tax.

For politicians to put Social Security in the same unfunded entitlements as health care is a big lie. Social Security may have an adjustment in 2017; however, the health care entitlements will bankrupt the U.S. Treasury in 2010.

In 2005, the financial report of the United States says the U.S. federal deficit was $318.5 billion plus $175 billion taken from the Social Security Trust Fund.

So the true federal deficit in 2005 was not $319 billion but $494 billion. I don't mind the U.S. government spending the Social Security surplus to lessen their true budget deficits; however, I detest the fact that they haven't leveled with the American people that since 1983 the government has spent $3 trillion of Social Security money.

The federal budget is in near bankruptcy; the health care system is an entitlement which will put a few nails in the coffin of the federal budget. However, the Social Security system is well financed and can meet its obligations in the future.

Don't let politicians tell you how they are going to fix the Social Security system. Social Security is the last thing that needs fixing.

44

PUBLISHED MAY 24, 2003

VISA PERMITS DRIVE DOWN WAGES AND TAKE AWAY AMERICAN JOBS

We the American people must demand FAIR WORLD TRADE to replace UNFAIR free world trade. In order to adopt a new FAIR world trade policy we must resign (GET OUT) of the WTO (World Trade Organization) immediately if not sooner.

This is the #1 issue in the 2004 presidential campaign.

I am reprinting this letter.

Visa program gives American jobs to aliens

To the Editor:
Most Americans have never heard of the H-1B visa program. But a growing number of high-tech engineers, programmers and electronics specialists have found out about it the hard way.

In 1990, Congress and President Bush (the elder) created the program, which allows variously skilled foreigners to enter the United States. In the year 2000 alone, 355,605 arrived and accepted lower pay for jobs that were taken away from Americans. Since the program began, between 800,000 and 1 million jobs have been lost to foreign workers. Ask someone who has been replaced by a foreigner with a "temporary" H-1B visa and you'll discover that it's not temporary.

H-1B isn't the only program some firms are using to reduce their payrolls with foreign workers. Companies possessing an overseas division can funnel workers hired outside our country into jobs here in the United States with L-1 visas, another program favoring outsiders over Americans. There were 294,658 L-1 visas granted in the year 2000.

Congress should be told to abolish both the H-1B and L-1 visa programs, not only to keep jobs of Americans from being taken by non-citizens but to maintain America's leadership as a first world power.

William McNally, Windham

45

PUBLISHED SEPT. 4, 2003

WHY I AM SUING THE NH DEMOCRATIC PARTY

First, I am reprinting Richard Driscoll's letter to the editor, 8/19/03.

Conned into giving our jobs and nation away

To the Editors: We have been conned into giving away our nation. No nation has ever maintained its standard of living or a prominent position in the world once it has lost its industrial base.

The United States is rapidly losing its industrial base, it is losing its manufacturing jobs, it is losing its high-tech jobs, and it is losing its ability to be self-sufficient, all with the blessings of both political parties. Not one candidate for the office of President of the United States has stated that if elected he would stop this hemorrhaging of American jobs to overseas locations.

Richard Driscoll
Plaistow

IF the NH DEMOCRATIC PARTY HAD NOT SHUT ME OUT OF THE NATIONAL PRESIDENTIAL CAMPAIGN AND DEBATES, MR. DRISCOLL WOULD HAVE KNOWN I AM A CANDIDATE FOR PRESIDENT WHOSE MAIN ISSUE IS TO STABILIZE AND REBUILD OUR MANUFACTURING AND HI-TECH INDUSTRIES.

There are MILLIONS OF RICHARD DRISCOLLS in AMERICA WHO WILL VOTE FOR ME BECAUSE OF MY ISSUES IF THEY KNOW OF ME.

WILL A RISING STOCK MARKET BRING PROSPERITY?

The stock market BOASTS 10,000, the Wall Street TV analysts say HAPPY DAYS ARE HERE AGAIN, the RECESSION IS OVER and the ECONOMY HAS RECOVERED, they say, while AMERICA KEEPS LOSING JOBS.

What's happening in the stock market is companies are making money BY CUTTING JOBS AT HOME and EXPORTING AMERICAN JOBS TO FOREIGN COUNTRIES in order to show profits for their investors.

Those INVESTORS, who will make money when the stock market is up in the 10,000s, will eventually LOSE THEIR SHIRTS in the stock market. Serves them right for NOT TAKING STOCK IN AMERICA. While ignoring the job losses in the American economy, they greedily pursued the almighty buck.

THE STOCK MARKET HAS NOTHING TO DO WITH PROSPERITY

PROSPERITY in the American economy will ONLY COME when we STABILIZE AND REBUILD our MANUFACTURING and HI-TECH INDUSTRIES. PROSPERITY will come when we give AMERICAN CITIZENS THE JOBS that are RIGHTFULLY THEIRS in what is still THE GREATEST ECONOMY IN THE WORLD, OUR AMERICAN ECONOMY.

THE GNP IS ANOTHER LEADING ECONOMIC INDICATOR WHICH DOES NOT BRING PROSPERITY

The GNP (Gross National Product) is the OFFICIAL INDEX our government uses to ASSESS PROSPERITY.

One would think that the GNP would be the TOTAL VOLUME OF GOODS manufactured in America, but it isn't.

The GNP measures only activity, it measures neither prosperity nor well being. The GNP only measures activities in the formal economy, WHICH GIVES RISE to a MONETARY TRANSACTION.

So in essence, floods, forest fires, increased crime, which necessitates more law officers, homeland security, blackouts and many other NEGATIVE things ALL ADD TO OUR GNP.

Now our government tells us the GNP is going to rise 2 TO 3% in the SECOND HALF of this year and WE AMERICANS WILL ALL PROSPER as the economic recovery WILL PUT AMERICANS BACK TO WORK. Happy days are here again – what a bunch of BULL-CRAP.

IT'S TOMORROW, WHERE ARE THE JOBS?

In 1964, I went into the post office in Rochester, N.H., and there was a new picture of our President, Lyndon Baines Johnson. Under his picture was the caption "YOU CAN'T HAVE TOMORROW'S JOB WITH TODAY'S SKILLS. GO TO THE COLLEGE OF YOUR CHOICE."

Thirty to 40 percent of this year's college graduates CANNOT FIND JOBS. Next year, 50 TO 60 PERCENT of the graduating college students WILL NOT BE ABLE TO FIND JOBS.

SO MUCH FOR FREE WORLD TRADE, WHICH IS A BUNCH OF BULL-CRAP.

46

PUBLISHED OCT. 2, 2003

WE HAVE A DEPARTMENT OF HOMELAND SECURITY TO FIGHT TERRORISM – WE NEED A NEW AGENCY TO STABILIZE AND REBUILD OUR AMERICAN ECONOMY

I, being the ONLY BUSINESSMAN running for President, have FORESIGHT in regards to our American economy while the President and 10 major Democratic presidential candidates have nothing but HINDSIGHT.

I see our economy (fiscal year ending 9/30/03) and our next fiscal year ending 9/30/04 being a false economy propelled by DEFICIT SPENDING close to $1 trillion in both years.

In BUSINESS they say an economy without a balanced budget is a FALSE ECONOMY, just like a family living well beyond their means.

The President and the Republican administration are telling us our economy is growing and that WITH THEIR TAX CUTS that JOBS will soon be coming. NOTHING COULD BE FURTHER FROM THE TRUTH.

America has been participating in a RIGGED GAME called FREE WORLD TRADE for many years now. We need a NEW AGENCY in America to STABILIZE AND REBUILD AMERICAN JOBS IN OUR AMERICAN ECONOMY. We can NO LONGER let our trading partners (friend or foe) UNFAIRLY MILK OUR COUNTRY OF THE JOBS WE NEED TO PAY THE TAXES that America needs to pay for our military, our health care, our education, our Social Security, our welfare system, our food stamps, our fuel assistance, etc., etc., etc.

The 10 Democratic presidential hopefuls have NO CLUE in regards to what needs to be done to SAVE OUR ECONOMY. They all offer BAND-AID SOLUTIONS for our ailing economy when it needs a major operation before our vital signs pronounce our dying economy dead.

BEFORE I GET INTO SOME OF THE DUTIES OF MY NEW ECONOMIC SECURITY AGENCY, I WANT TO REPRINT THIS 9/18 NEWS BULLETIN AND GIVE MY OBSERVATIONS ON IT.

OPEC recognizes Iraq's interim council

The U.S.-appointed interim government for Iraq will get a boost in the international community next week when the Organization of Petroleum Exporting Countries welcomes an Iraqi delegation for the first time since the war. Reintegration of OPEC is a big step on Iraq's path toward normalized international relations because of the importance of of oil to its economy and to the success of its interim government. Iraq's oil minister, Ibrahim Mohamed Bahr al-Uloum, will attend the OPEC meeting Sept. 24 in Vienna.

SURPRISE – SURPRISE

It's no news to me as a BUSINESSMAN that OPEC wants Iraq to join their MONOPOLISTIC OIL CARTEL CALLED OPEC.

Just imagine the economic input to the American economy IF IRAQI OIL could be produced to their MAXIMUM CAPABILITIES. That would destroy OPEC's monopolistic supply of oil and bring much lower and STABLE PRICES to America and the rest of the world.

So IF the OPEC CARTEL WAS BROKEN, Americans would have more money to spend in our economy without being forced to pay most of our disposable income on HIGH GAS PRICES and HIGH HEATING OIL.

So we MUST send our TROOPS to Iraq and Afghanistan to secure the borders (this will save AMERICAN LIVES) and secure the oil pipelines to open the Iraq oil business to its MAXIMUM PRODUCTIVITY.

HERE ARE A FEW OF THE DRASTIC MEASURES THE NEW ECONOMIC AGENCY NEEDS TO ADDRESS:

1. Put the AMERICAN economy BEFORE the GLOBAL economy by withdrawing from international organizations that THREATEN OUR SOVEREIGNTY and ECONOMIC INDEPENDENCE.

2. BREAK OPEN foreign markets to American products with RECIPROCAL TRADE TREATIES.

3. Oppose fast track authority as a unilateral surrender by Congress of its constitutional power to amend trade treaties. THE PRESIDENT SHOULD NOT HAVE FAST TRACK TRADE AUTHORITY.

4. Resist expansion or extension of NAFTA and GATT.

5. Push for WITHDRAWAL FROM THE WTO and a return to BILATERAL TRADE TREATIES enforced by the U.S. and its trade partners.

6. Protect vital American industries by passing and enforcing TOUGH ANTI-DUMPING LEGISLATION.

7. Impose tariffs on foreign imports equal to the taxes imposed on goods made in the U.S. and use the revenue to cut American income taxes OR BALANCE THE FEDERAL BUDGET.

8. Etc., etc., etc.

THERE IS NO LIGHT AT THE END OF THE TUNNEL IN REGARDS TO OUR ECONOMY. CONTINUED JOB LOSSES AT HOME WILL, IN A FEW YEARS, DESTROY OUR STANDARD OF LIVING, BRING ON GREATER TAXATION, TAKE AWAY MORE OF OUR FREEDOMS AND CREATE CIVIL VIOLENCE IN MOST ALL AMERICAN CITIES.

47

PUBLISHED AUG. 23, 2006

SLAP A 20 PERCENT TARIFF ON ALL IMPORTS FROM CHINA

Our President and our Congress lack three ingredients to effectively deal with Communist China. The ingredients are the intestinal fortitude (guts), backbone, and business experience.

For several years now, Communist China has broken every free trade agreement ever written. Along with these broken trade agreements, they have an unlimited workforce that works for two or three dollars an hour. That alone gives them a yearly trade imbalance with America of about $200 billion a year.

Now, to add insult to injury, they devalue their currency about 20 percent less than it should be against the American dollar. So in essence, they are taking our jobs and taking investment from America to China, which also takes our jobs.

This 20 percent artificial devaluation of their Chinese currency costs America $80 billion a year. Let's see now, if we have a trade imbalance of $200 billion a year and 20 percent of that is $40 billion, am I wrong?

Our U.S. Congress and the Bush administration high officials have been trying to get Communist China to take their 20 percent devaluation off, but to no avail. China is bargaining from a position of strength because they are one of America's primary lenders and they also hold $407 billion in U.S. Treasury bonds and over $1 trillion ready to buy up America.

Little wonder why 70 percent of the Chinese are learning how to speak English. This is NO joke, but China's second language SHOULD BE Spanish, so they can boss around all the Mexicans who can't speak English who are living in America.

Now let's get serious. America must immediately slap a 20 percent tariff on all Chinese imports. This tariff will stand until they stop devaluing their currency by 20 percent. In tennis, this could be called 40 to 40 or deuce. However, the ball is in China's court. It's their serve.

If the President, Karl Rove, I mean George W. Bush, and the do-nothing Congress had any business sense, they would call China's bluff.

Although China is our bank (they are the lender and we are the borrower) they still need us more than we need them. We can't negotiate with Communist China; we must play hardball with them.

We can, on a given time table, pay off our $407 billion in treasury notes and we can get other suppliers world-wide and in the good old USA to supply our economy with the goods it needs. Will retail prices go up? Yes, but the quality of our goods will last longer.

We made Communist China a super power economically and they are well on their way to becoming a military super power. At the same time, we won't give Socialistic/Communist Cuba the right time.

Along with making China a most favored nation each year we asked them to do better on human rights and not to spread nuclear technology to any third world country.

Guess who made Pakistan a nuclear-armed nation? The answer is China. The so-called Cold War is over; however, both Communist China and Russia are spreading nuclear arms around the world for capitalistic monetary gains.

We must brace China right now with a 20 percent tariff, for within a year it may be too late.

48

PUBLISHED MAY 10, 2007

FREE MARKET SYSTEM IS BROKEN

In the free enterprise system, we are told that the price of a certain commodity is governed by the law of supply and demand. Oil is SUPPOSEDLY in short supply, and the demand is at an all-time high, thus we have high gas prices.

Well, I only went to high school but I can tell you that the law of supply and demand does not work when too few control the supply or too few control the demand. The fact that OPEC, which only contributes 17 percent of all the world's crude oil, can monopolistically control the supply leads me to ask: Where are the other 83 percent who control five times more crude oil than OPEC?

The answer is that the 83 percent are not competing in price for a portion of the world oil market but rather are playing follow-the-leader prices set by OPEC. As I mentioned earlier, the law of supply and demand doesn't work when too few control the supply or demand.

Not only do OPEC and the 83 percent of others control the crude oil but they, and the large oil companies, control the refineries which control the inventory of our refined gas and heating oil.

If that isn't enough monopolistic pricing powers, the large oil companies control the retail gas stations and engage in non-competitive retail price fixing at the gas stations. There are a few areas in America where there is still some competition in price; that's why prices in some states are lower than most of the other states.

So the law of supply and demand doesn't work when too few control the supply or the demand, which leads to no competition in the drilling, refining and retailing of crude oil.

The fact that our Congress and our President can say gas prices and heating oil prices are a result of free market supply and demand is beyond comprehension. They say if we decrease our demand that prices will fall.

No way will gas and oil prices go down if we in the U.S. decrease our demand. We are between a rock and a hard place. The rock is OPEC and the other 83 percent of the monopolistic cartel and the hard place is their partners – the big oil companies. Too few control the supply (OPEC) and too few control the wholesale and retail distribution of that supply.

Present gas prices and the prospect of higher gas prices will put the U.S. economy into DEFLATION within a year. The American consumer will have little or no money to purchase other goods and services needed to sustain our economy, never mind grow our economy.

America must create competition for OPEC and the large oil companies. We must build, as soon as possible, five or six huge (non-profit) refineries. With our U.S. refineries building up our inventories, we will not face shortages or fear of shortages. We then could sell our refined gas to large national retail chains like Wal-Mart to bring competition in price to the retail section of the oil industry.

If America cannot free ourselves from the monopolistic pricing powers of OPEC and the large oil companies, we will not be able to control our own economic destiny.

Throughout this guest commentary I have stated that the laws of supply and demand don't work when too few control the supply or too few control the demand. Make no mistake about it; we in America, along with China, Japan and the European Community, do control the DEMAND. By controlling the demand we can restore competition back into the crude oil industry.

Remember, they need our dollars as much as we need their oil.

If anyone has read this far in my commentary and come to the conclusion that America cannot build non-profit (government owned) refineries, I say we can't continue with our massive trade deficits, budget deficits, declining dollar, and the possibility of deflation or a recession in our American economy.

49

PUBLISHED MARCH 31, 2008

THE DECADE OF 1970 HAD A 100% INFLATION RATE CAUSED BY BIG LABOR & BIG BUSINESS

I am writing in reference to your *(Foster's Daily Democrat)* March 10 editorial, "No quick fix is on the way." The subheading on this editorial was "Bernanke may soon have to say stop stagflation."

To set the record straight, we did not experience stagflation in the decade of the 1970s. What we had in the '70s was inflation caused by the power of the big labor unions to demand and receive wages and benefits that far exceeded their productivity. Big business simply applied follow-the-leader price increases, causing inflation.

Whereas the standard definition for inflation is too much money chasing too few goods and services, the inflation of the 1970s was caused by labor and big business. How did the big labor unions and the big businesses get into this envious position where big labor could receive wage and benefit increases each year and big business could make profits by simply raising prices?

Well, we have to go back to 1968, where LBJ let the airline industry receive a 19 percent wage and benefits contract. Until that time, JFK had the Kennedy wage and price guidelines in effect. Big labor could not navigate any contract exceeding 6 percent per year and big business could not raise prices more than 6 percent per year.

During his time in office, Kennedy and his successor, LBJ, held big labor and big business within the 6 percent Kennedy guidelines. The business world was watching LBJ who, with his jawboning power and the withholding of government contracts, could have stopped the 19 percent airlines contract which broke the 6 percent Kennedy wage and price guidelines. LBJ, because of 1968 congressional elections, chose to do the politically popular thing, which was to let the airlines' union break the Kennedy 6 percent wage and benefit guidelines.

So, what started out as a wage and benefit inflation became a price and wage inflation as big business raised their prices before uncovering wage union contracts. This resulted in yearly inflation rates of 10 percent or more and 100 percent inflation for the decade of the 1970s.

Needless to say, we had to stop inflation. They had to raise interest rates to 10 percent or more each year in the 1970s, so whereas big business did not have to invest money to increase productivity, they simply made profits by raising prices. The decade of the 1970s was not stagflation. It was inflation caused by big business and big labor.

The only similarity between the 1970s and today is that many middle and lower income Americans, whose wages and benefits are not keeping pace with inflation, cannot purchase as many goods and services or pay as much taxes.

In the decade of the 1970s the inflationary cost of living went up equally for all Americans; however, the wages and benefits of many non-union workers did not receive wage increases.

Americans were pushed into the lower income wage earners. Yes, the 1970s did much to decrease the number of Americans who are today called the middle class.

So in 2008, 2009 and 2010 we will not have stagflation or inflation. We will have a recession, which many will call a depression. Many Americans will not be able to put food on the table, gas in their gas tank and pay ever increasing state and federal taxes.

If you were a non-union worker in January 1970 and your wages were $200 a week, your wages and benefits (if you had any) must have risen to $400 per week on Jan. 1, 1980. The inflation rate for the decade was 100 percent, so the cost of living went up 100 percent for everyone. So if at the beginning of January 1970 your wages were $200 per week and on Jan. 1, 1980 your wages were $240 a week, your standard of living went down $60 per week.

So the decade of the 1970s did much to lower the standard of living for America's lower and middle income Americans.

Isn't it ironic that today the airlines who broke the 6 percent Kennedy wage and price guidelines want we the taxpayers to guarantee their pensions, which were between their labor unions and big business?

No way should the U.S. taxpayers guarantee their pensions.

50

PUBLISHED FEB. 1, 2007

GDP IS NOT A MEASURE OF PROSPERITY

Our government and the media tell us Americans that our economy is good and strong. The basis of this assumption is that the GDP (Gross Domestic Product) has grown an average of 3 to 4 percent each quarter for several years.

True, the GDP has grown; however, the GDP is not a measure of prosperity nor well-being of the American people. In a good economy, most all Americans should be able to make ends meet and even save some money.

Today, in this false economy, more and more Americans are getting deeper and deeper in debt and cannot save any money. Also, our federal government in this so-called good economy cannot balance the budget. (In 2005, the deficit was $319 billion, plus the Social Security surplus of $175 billion equals a $494 billion deficit. America paid $327 billion in interest in 2005.)

Whereas the GDP measures all monetary transactions in the American economy, not all money accounted for in the GDP is good for the American economy and certainly not good for the majority of Americans who are not rich or poor.

So if the GDP goes up 3-1/2 percent the first quarter after the Katrina hurricane and many other negative things push the GDP up, how can an increase in the GDP be the barometer for calling the American economy strong?

In this commentary, I am not suggesting that the GDP figures are not helpful in measuring the strength of our economy; I am only trying to say that there is a better way to determine whether we truly have a strong economy or not.

I say we have a strong economy when the majority of us Americans (not the 10 percent higher income or the 30 percent lower income and poor) can pay all our taxes, purchase cars and homes, and not need any of the government taxpayer programs to make their living.

So when the majority of us Americans can pay our taxes, purchase high ticket goods and services and do not use any government (taxpayer) money, we are ASSETS to a good economy in which the federal government should balance their budget.

So now that we know that Americans who pay their taxes, purchase goods and services, and do not need help from the government are assets to the economy, who are the liabilities?

When our federal government tells us they have created over 7.2 million new jobs, what they don't say is that the great majority of these jobs are liabilities to our economy. These jobs pay so little that these 7.2 million new employees pay little or no taxes, purchase no high ticket goods and services, and use every taxpayer government program that is available to the American poor and the illegal immigrants as well.

So as the assets to the American economy get few and fewer and the liabilities get higher and higher, America's true economy gets weaker and weaker.

Instead of using the GDP as a measuring stick for our economy, we should get quarterly reports of the number of American workers who are assets to our economy. If we can maintain or grow our assets then the economy will be a true economy, not one built on increasing consumer debt and increasing federal deficits.

If America continues to lose good paying jobs (assets) and increases low paying jobs (liabilities), our American economy will get weaker and weaker, even if the GDP grows and grows.

51

PUBLISHED MAY 31, 2007

RIGAZIO ENDORSES KUCINICH

The Chinese government has its currency undervalued by 40 percent. With the ever-growing trade imbalance with China, the U.S. has to pay China the difference in this trade increase in U.S. dollars.

China also breaks all the other rules of fair trade, and the WTO (World Trade Organization) just lets them continue their unfair trade practices.

As William Ross (CEO of many new American companies who were once defunct) said several years ago, the WTO is a WEALTH TRANSFER ORGANIZATION, heavily weighted against America, and the problem of free world trade is that only America practices it.

Just how does the WTO transfer wealth? It's really quite simple. They let foreign countries take away the good jobs of the American citizens. Make no mistake about it; Americans with good jobs are our wealth. They pay the most taxes, purchase high ticket goods and services, and use no taxpayer programs intended for America's poor and illegal immigrants.

The first thing America should do is slap a 40 percent tariff on all Chinese imports. That will get their attention and make them realize that they need us as much as we need them.

Every time many Americans (like me) insist on fair world trade we are called protectionists. We are not protectionists; we just want reciprocal trade agreements.

Economists call our economy UNSTABLE. So sooner or later there has got to be a halt in these ever-growing trade imbalances, which are the root cause of our budget deficits.

The WTO is a secret unelected organization, which is supposed to be the last phase of globalization after NAFTA and GATT. Before globalization, America used to be the cream of the milk bottle, and globalization has homogenized us. I am just concerned that we do not become the skim milk in the bottle.

The only presidential candidate who wants out of the WTO is Congressman Dennis Kucinich. He has already got my maximum donation to his campaign. He also has my official endorsement – that, along with 50 cents, will buy you a Pepsi Cola in some places.

52

PUBLISHED NOV. 22, 2007

DEBATE IS MORE POLITICAL THEATER

It's Friday morning, and I must give my commentary on the Thursday night Democratic Debate.

As usual, it was more political theater than getting any real information as to what these candidates for President will do to balance the federal budget and start to pay down our national debt.

A second tier candidate got very little attention and was totally ignored in the media after the so-called debate. If the general public could think for themselves, they would have realized that Dennis Kucinich and Senator Joe Biden were by far the most informed and by far the most honest, answering the questions without making short political speeches.

I have been in the Kucinich corner since 2004, when I was in the Republican Presidential NH Primary. Mostly because of his positions on so-called free trade agreements, which are taking away millions of good American jobs with no end in sight.

That being said, I think Senator Joe Biden, with his 35 years of experience, is more than qualified to be President of the U.S. He understands the complexity of our nation's problems which must be contained before they become a crisis, which many problems have already become.

I am going to vote for Kucinich in the NH primaries; however, I will vote for Hillary in the 2008 general election. She is going to be our next President, and Joe Biden (if he would accept) would be a great Vice President on her ticket.

Maybe Bill Clinton and Joe Biden could be a big influence on Hillary's monumental decisions that she must make to rebuild the damage done by President Bush's "Deficits don't matter" economic policy, which has doubled the national debt in his two terms in office.

53

PUBLISHED OCT. 23, 2003

POLITICAL REALITY #1

IF you had a POLITICAL AGENDA such as I have, WHAT BETTER WAY to get YOUR MESSAGE out to the American people than having YOUR NAME ON THE BALLOT FOR PRESIDENT OF THE UNITED STATES in NH's, FIRST IN THE NATION PRIMARY?

It is EASY to have your name on the ballot. One must be either a Democrat or a Republican, then fill out a simple form and then give the NH Secretary of State a check for $1,000.

I was, UNTIL APRIL of this year, an undeclared or INDEPENDENT as it used to be called. I changed my voter registration to Democrat to run for president as a Democrat.

This week I have gone to the city hall in Barrington, NH and changed my voter registration to REPUBLICAN and will run for president as a REPUBLICAN.

In my opinion, the American economy is in a CRISIS PERIOD and whether you're a Democrat, Republican, Liberal, Conservative, or Moderate IS IRRELEVANT.

What is RELEVANT is that we need a department of HOMELAND SECURITY FOR OUR ECONOMY. We must PASS AND ENFORCE LAWS TO PROTECT THE JOBS of AMERICAN WORKERS IN OUR OWN AMERICAN ECONOMY.

In order to do this, we must GET OUT OF THE WTO (World Trade Organization) which William Ross, a new CEO of a new American Steel Company, said, "THE WTO IS A WEALTH TRANSFER ORGANIZATION WHOSE INTERESTS ARE HEAVILY WEIGHTED AGAINST THE U.S. INTERESTS AND THE TERRIBLE FLAW IN FREE WORLD TRADE IS THAT ONLY AMERICA PRACTICES IT."

POLITICAL REALITY #2

A vote for me as a Republican in the Jan. 27 primaries would be sending President Bush a message and would be kind of a PROTEST VOTE of his ECONOMIC POLICIES and his PHASE II handling of the GUERILLA WAR NOW TAKING PLACE IN IRAQ.

I also would hope that some of my answers to America's problems would be CONSIDERED by the Republican and Democratic administrations or at the very least CHANGE PUBLIC OPINION ON MANY OF THE ISSUES.

It's the Democratic and Republican Parties who work hard in the primaries to elect THEIR PARTY'S CANDIDATES. It's WE INDEPENDENTS WHO SHOULD STUDY THE ISSUES AND GET INVOLVED IN BACKING A CANDIDATE who they BELIEVE IN, whether that candidate is a FRONT RUNNER or one who is being IGNORED BY THE PRESS.

POLITICAL REALITY #3

The candidate to beat President Bush in 2004 MUST BE A DEMOCRAT. No splinter party or third party has a chance to be elected president and will only hurt the Democratic Party more than the Republican Party.

SO I AM ASKING ALL DEMOCRATS AND INDEPENDENTS TO VOTE FOR DENNIS J. KUCINICH.

Dennis is the ONLY DEMOCRATIC CANDIDATE who advocates the United States GETTING OUT OF NAFTA and the WTO (World Trade Organization). His positions on HEALTH CARE and SOCIAL SECURITY are the same sound COMMON SENSE principles as I have.

IF his position on Iraq were the same as mine I WOULD WITHDRAW from the presidential primary and back Dennis 100 percent.

HOWEVER, only time will tell whose position on Iraq is right (his or mine).

So I am running for President as a Republican, but I am going to back Dennis J. Kucinich as my choice on the Democratic side of the ballot.

Here are just some of the SO-CALLED RADICAL measures that my new Department of Homeland Security for the economy should address.

1. Put the AMERICAN economy BEFORE the GLOBAL economy by withdrawing from international organizations that THREATEN OUR SOVEREIGNTY and ECONOMIC INDEPENDENCE.

2. BREAK OPEN foreign markets to American products with RECIPROCAL TRADE TREATIES.

3. Oppose fast track authority as a unilateral surrender by Congress of its constitutional power to amend trade treaties. THE PRESIDENT SHOULD NOT HAVE FAST TRACK TRADE AUTHORITY.

4. Resist expansion or extension of NAFTA and GATT.

5. Push for WITHDRAWAL FROM THE WTO and a return to BILATERAL TRADE TREATIES enforced by the U.S. and its trade partners.

6. Protect vital American industries by passing and enforcing TOUGH ANTI-DUMPING LEGISLATION.

7. Impose tariffs on foreign imports equal to the taxes imposed on goods made in the U.S. and use the revenue to cut American income taxes OR BALANCE THE FEDERAL BUDGET.

8. Etc., etc., etc.

THERE IS NO LIGHT AT THE END OF THE TUNNEL IN REGARDS TO OUR ECONOMY. CONTINUED JOB LOSSES AT HOME WILL, IN A FEW YEARS, DESTROY OUR STANDARD OF LIVING, BRING ON GREATER TAXATION, TAKE AWAY MORE OF OUR FREEDOMS AND CREATE CIVIL VIOLENCE IN MOST ALL AMERICAN CITIES.

54

PUBLISHED SEPT. 20, 2007

VICK DESERVES A SECOND CHANCE

Michael Vick pleaded guilty to financing and participating in illegal dog fighting matches, upon which huge amounts of money were bet. He awaits sentencing later this month.

I have a question and an observation to make. Why are illegal dog fighting matches so widespread across America? Could it be that officials at the town, city and even state level are being paid off to keep a blind eye to these events?

My observation is that if local authorities had not allowed dog fighting matches, Michael Vick would not have been able to participate in these illegal dog fighting matches.

As a judge, I would give Michael Vick a two-year jail term (suspended) and a two-year term working with cruelty to animals organizations. Also, after a year, he should be allowed to go back in the NFL. Everyone deserves a second chance.

Michael Vick's prosecution will bring much heat on the dog fighting matches which still occur in America. That alone should be a great benefit to society.

Yes, Michael brought dog fighting out of the shadows and has dealt dog fighting matches a great blow, if not stopping them altogether in America. For this we all owe Michael Vick a vote of thanks.

As an afterthought, you must have heard the much repeated slogan on TV – "It's not the size of the dog in the fight, it's the size of the fight in the dog" – which must have been referring to illegal dog fights where a smaller dog sometimes maims or kills a larger dog.

If society had been doing its job preventing illegal dog fights, Michael Vick would probably have bought a couple of thoroughbred race horses to bet on.

55

THANK YOU, MARGARET TILLINGHAST

I read the daily newspapers and watch TV news programs. I consider myself pretty well informed on what's happening to America.

I was aware of the FAST TRACK legislation called Presidential Trade Promotion Authority. However, I DID NOT READ ANYWHERE in the media WHAT this piece of legislation MEANT to America and to our ability to control our own ECONOMIC DESTINY in the near future.

I am, at MY OWN EXPENSE, reprinting Margaret's letter to the editor for ALL AMERICANS to read, so they may call their congressmen to VOTE NO on the Presidential Trade Promotion Authority. Let's DERAIL this FAST TRACK legislation, which is in the best interests of the WTO (World Trade Organization) and NOT IN THE BEST INTERESTS OF AMERICA AND THE AMERICAN PEOPLE.

TO THE EDITOR

In the midst of our national grief, many fail to recognize the threat to our democracy explained by the following letter:

By stealthy and clever tactics, a coup is under way that can deal a body blow to our democracy. The coup is in the form of a trade agreement that will supersede present U.S. law and become law for every country in the Americas, except Cuba. It is wrapped in rosy promises of dedication to democracy and a better life for all, and has an innocuous-sounding title, "Free Trade Area of the Americas" (FTAA).

The rosy promises have no teeth, but the essence of the agreement has very sharp teeth. The essence includes a startling reversal of the right of government to regulate business for the benefit of the public. Over the years our government, through democratically passed laws, ended child labor, established the 40-hour week, assured a safe food supply, and much more. To enforce those laws, government could fine businesses.

The FTAA turns things upside down. Corporations can sue governments for passing any law that would be a barrier to their present or potential future profits. Suits will be settled, not by the courts, but by three-person tribunals meeting in secret. The value of a law for the well-being of people or the environment is irrelevant to the tribunal. Judgment is based solely on how much profit would be lost. Fines can be sufficiently huge to force governments to rescind laws.

So much for government of, by, and for the people.

The giant corporations leading this coup know that an informed public would not support it, so they want Congress to approve the FTAA by a special "fast track" legislative process that would eliminate public hearings with expert testimony, prohibit amendments, and limit debate.

The vote on "fast track" (now called "Presidential Trade Promotion Authority") may come soon. Please ask Smith, Gregg, Bass and Sununu to oppose "fast track" and uphold the right and duty of Congress to hold public hearings, consider amendments and allow thorough debate.

Margaret Tillinghast and others
Durham

AGAIN, THANK YOU MARGARET

What I would like to know is what OUR NH CONGRESSMEN think about the Free Trade Area of the Americas (FTAA) and the fast track Presidential Trade Promotion Authority???

If our NH Congressional leaders DO NOT INFORM their CONSTITUENTS (NH citizens) about FTAA and the Presidential Trade Authority we SHOULD vote them OUT OF OFFICE IN 2002 AND 2004.

56

PUBLISHED OCTOBER 2003

THE TRAP

In 1993, Sir James Goldsmith wrote a book entitled *The Trap*. This book was a #1 BEST SELLER IN FRANCE IN 1993. The book tells in DETAIL how the large multinational corporations were going to GLOBALIZE WORLD TRADE.

It's 10 years since *The Trap* was written and everything written in *The Trap* is forecasted 100 percent correctly. I call my copy of *The Trap,* which I have had for 10 years, MY BIBLE ON GLOBALIZATION and the CONSEQUENCES we the American people will have to pay when they bang the FINAL NAIL IN THE COFFIN CALLED GLOBALIZATION.

Last week, when President Bush visited France, there was an ANTI-GLOBALIZATION DEMONSTRATION in France which drew 20,000 people. We saw it for about FIVE SECONDS on national TV.

Make no mistake about it, when the WTO (World Trade Organization) sanctions the closing of a French manufacturing plant to BE RELOCATED in China or Vietnam, the French will take to the streets and totally paralyze the whole French economy.

What are we doing in America while the multinational corporations are taking away our manufacturing and high tech jobs? We are just sitting back and watching until we become a 100 percent service industry economy. Well, I for one AM MAD AS HELL AND I AM NOT GOING TO TAKE IT ANYMORE. That's why I am RUNNING FOR PRESIDENT OF THE UNITED STATES.

I AM REPRINTING TWO QUESTIONS ASKED TO GOLDSMITH IN 1993.

Who will be the losers and who will be the winners under a system of global free trade?

The losers will, of course, be those people who become unemployed as a result of production being moved to low-cost areas. There will also be those who lose their jobs because their employers do not move offshore and are not able to compete with cheap imported products. Finally, there will be those whose earning capacity is reduced following the shift in the sharing of value-added away from labor.

The winners will be those who can benefit from an almost inexhaustible supply of very cheap labor. They will be the companies who move their production off-shore to low-cost areas; the companies who can pay lower salaries at home; and those who have capital to invest where labor is cheapest, and who as a result will receive larger dividends. But they will be like the winners of a poker game on the *Titanic.* The wounds inflicted on their societies will be too deep, and brutal consequences could follow.

The new phenomenon of our age is the emergence of transnational corporations, with the ability to move production at will anywhere in the world, in order to systematically benefit from lower wages wherever they are to be found. Transnational corporations now account for one-third of global output; their global annual sales have reached $4.8 trillion, which is greater than total international trade. The largest 100 multinational corporations control about one-third of all foreign direct investment. The globalization of the market is vital to them, both to produce cheaply and to sell universally. Because they do not necessarily owe allegiance to the countries where they operate, there is a divorce between the interests of the transnational corporations and those of society.

You must remember that one of the characteristics of developing countries is that a small handful of people control the overwhelming majority of the nation's resources. It is these people who own most of their nation's industrial, commercial and financial enterprises and who assemble the cheap labor which is used to manufacture products for the developed world. Thus, it is the poor in the rich countries who will subsidize the rich in the poor countries. This will have a serious impact on the social cohesion of nations.

What are your thoughts about the World Trade Organization?

That is the organization which is supposed to replace GATT, regulate international trade, and lead us to global economic integration. It is yet another international bureaucracy whose functionaries will be largely autonomous. They report to over 120 nations and therefore, in practice, to nobody. Each nation will have one vote out of 120. Thus, America and every European nation will be handing over ultimate control of its economic destiny to an unelected, uncontrolled group of international bureaucrats.

WAKE UP, AMERICANS; LET'S NOT LET THE LARGE MULTINATIONAL CORPORATIONS CONTROL OUR OWN ECONOMIC DESTINY.

I will be putting my message on the Internet and I will SPEAK at any Democratic Party convention and I am also available to speak at ANY civic organization. PLEASE HELP ME in sending my message: "STOP GLOBALIZATION before we Americans have a much LOWER standard of living, increased taxation, less and less freedoms, and internal revolutions in many American cities."

57

PUBLISHED SEPTEMBER 2003

IT IS REAGAN, BUSH SR., AND PRESIDENT GEORGE W. BUSH (REPUBLICANS) WHO ARE RESPONSIBLE FOR OUR HUGE FEDERAL DEFICITS

President Reagan (1980-1988) increased military spending but DID NOT TAX THE PEOPLE for it, thus running up MUCH OF the nearly $7 trillion national debt we have today. One time president George Bush Sr. (1988-2002) tried to not raise taxes (READ MY LIPS) but had to raise taxes although NOT NEARLY ENOUGH.

Between Reagan and Bush Sr. they were accountable for $5 trillion of the increase in our national debt.

On top of this, they spent nearly $2 TRILLION in SOCIAL SECURITY SURPLUS. In the monthly financial reports in the newspapers (which stopped shortly after the Clinton administration took over) the public newspaper report would read in the month of October the federal deficit was $200 billion PLUS $60 billion of Social Security surplus.

Reagan and Bush Sr. wiped out all of the Social Security surplus. President Clinton (1992-2000), with HUGE TAX INCREASES and 8 YEARS OF FALSE GROWTH in the stock market, was able to BUILD UP the Social Security surplus.

ALONG COMES GEORGE W. BUSH

While campaigning for president he was going to take THE SURPLUS and GIVE IT BACK TO THE PEOPLE in the form of TAX CUTS. He also wanted to let the younger generation take some of their Social Security payments and let them invest in the STOCK MARKET.

President Bush DID NOT tell the people that the SURPLUS was SOCIAL SECURITY SURPLUS. Today as you read this political column the federal deficits are so large that the SOCIAL SECURITY SURPLUS IS ZERO and much of the Social Security current payments are being used for spending OTHER THAN SOCIAL SECURITY PAYMENTS.

The president wants to REFORM (semi-privatize) the Social Security system in order to get out of the $3 trillion that our government owes the Social Security program.

This $3 trillion our government owes the Social Security Trust Fund is (ACCORDING TO FORMER SECRETARY OF THE TREASURY PAUL O'NEIL) NOT EVEN ACCOUNTED FOR in the FEDERAL BOOKS. I guess if WE OWE IT TO OURSELVES it is a NON-ENTRY IN THE BOOKS.

THE FEDERAL GOVERNMENT IS NOT GOING TO REPAY THE SOCIAL SECURITY SURPLUS, SO I, JOHN DONALD RIGAZIO, DEMOCRATIC CANDIDATE FOR PRESIDENT, HAVE THE ANSWER TO KEEPING SOCIAL SECURITY INTACT.

(Step #1) In 2005, put ALL Social Security revenue into a SPECIAL SOCIAL SECURITY ACCOUNT which the U.S. government CANNOT use for any other purpose.

(Step #2) Unfortunately, we must increase workers' Social Security payments from 6.2 percent of their income to 8 percent. This, of course, means the EMPLOYERS' MATCHING SOCIAL SECURITY PAYMENTS also go up from 6.2 percent to 8 percent.

So in 2005 the Social Security payments from the workers is 8 percent and a matching 8 percent is now 16 percent compared to the 6.2 percent + 6.2 percent which equals 12.4 percent.

This increase of 3.6 percent will soon start generating a huge SOCIAL SECURITY SURPLUS.

(Step #3) We must INCREASE THE BASE of American workers who pay Social Security. I propose EVERY AMERICAN WORKER, CITIZEN OR NOT, must PAY INTO and receive Social Security when they become eligible.

IF the BUSH REPUBLICAN ADMINISTRATION LETS ANY YOUNG OR OLD AMERICAN WORKER TAKE ANY OF THEIR SOCIAL SECURITY PAYMENTS OUT OF THE GENERAL SOCIAL SECURITY POT, IT'S THE FIRST STEP TOWARD DISMANTLING THE CURRENT GOVERNMENT GUARANTEED SOCIAL SECURITY SYSTEM.

GEORGE W. BUSH'S (2004) BUDGET YEAR END 9/30/04

The president's 2004 budget is our expansionary budget. By that I mean his proposed $2.2 trillion IN SPENDING (which doesn't include the expenses in Iraq) is $304 billion MORE THAN OUR TOTAL FEDERAL REVENUES RECEIVED THE PREVIOUS YEAR.

It is of my businessman's VIEWPOINT that revenues for year ending 9/30/04 will be $500 to $600 BILLION LESS THAN THE PREVIOUS YEAR'S REVENUES. Of course, the $2.2 trillion in spending could be $2.5 trillion. The REASON THE REVENUES will be down is that BUSINESS PROFITS AND PERSONAL INCOME WILL BE WAY DOWN, thus we will have a $500 to $600 BILLION REVENUE SHORTFALL.

So it is of my opinion that the (2004) budget could not only be the projected $304 billion recognized in the EXPANSIONARY BUDGET but could reach nearly $1 trillion.

PRESIDENT BUSH'S VOODOO ECONOMICS

"Cut taxes, people have more money in their pockets, people spend more to buy things, this creates jobs." The SIMPLICITY of this Bush economic plan can only be matched by an uneducated person who, after going to three town meetings in which THE LOCAL DEFICIT was the main topic, took the floor and said, "I have been to three town meetings so far and that's all you have talked about is the DEFICIT. I suggest we SPEND THE DEFICIT and get on with new business."

58

PUBLISHED AUGUST 2003

IF I WERE PRESIDENT OF THE UNITED STATES

I wanted to go on national TV tonight and tell the American people that the WAR ON WORLD-WIDE TERRORISM IS JUST BEGINNING. It WILL NOT END until these COWARDLY TERRORIST GROUPS stop their suicide bombings, GUERILLA WARFARE and terrorist threats against America and our allies.

While we have removed the TALIBAN in Afghanistan and SADDAM HUSSEIN from Iraq, we still are COMMITTED to changing both their countries into FREE, SELF GOVERNED NATIONS.

There are STILL TERRORISTS in AFGHANISTAN and IRAQ who, through GUERILLA WARFARE, are TRYING TO STOP AMERICA FROM SUCCEEDING in setting up FREE, SELF-GOVERNED governments in these two countries WHO WERE IN CONTROL OF THESE TERRORISTS.

America WILL STICK TO OUR COMMITMENT IN CHANGING AFGHANISTAN AND IRAQ'S GOVERNMENTS INTO FREE, SELF-GOVERNED NATIONS. We must NOT let WORLD-WIDE TERRORISTS TAKE BACK CONROL OF AFGHANISTAN and IRAQ. If we do, it will be a great SETBACK to our war against GLOBAL TERRORISM.

With these facts said, I am redeploying many U.S. troops from South Korea and Germany and sending OUR MID-EAST GENERALS THE TROOPS THEY NEED TO TRACK DOWN AND KILL THESE TERRORISTS WHO ARE ENGAGING OUR TROOPS WITH GUERILLA WARFARE.

It has been 50 years or more since the Korean War and World War II. It's time South Korea and Germany (WHO WE MADE ECONOMIC SUPER POWERS) PROVIDE THEIR OWN GROUND TROOPS TO PROTECT THEIR OWN COUNTRIES.

Make no mistake about it, my fellow Americans; WE WILL be in Afghanistan and Iraq for years and yes, maybe DECADES because if there is a World War III it will BEGIN IN THE MID-EAST. That's THE BATTLEFRONT WE AMERICANS MUST BE PREPARED TO FIGHT.

In addition to sending more U.S. troops to Afghanistan and Iraq, I am ordering all National Guard in the military to be SENT HOME TO AMERICA. These National Guard soldiers could help protect OUR BORDERS and prevent terrorists from entering our country.

59

PUBLISHED SEPT. 6, 2001

YOU CAN'T "JUMP START" A DEAD BATTERY

The Federal Reserve board has given us seven interest rate cuts in the last year or so in an effort to create the SPARK which would fuel up the engine of the American economy.

The last ¼ percent interest rate cut DROPPED the stock market over 100 points on the day it was announced.

Although the battery which propelled our economy to nearly a decade of economic growth was probably a DIE-HARD BATTERY, it is now DEAD.

The American economy doesn't need any more "jump start" interest rate cuts, WE NEED A NEW BATTERY.

HOW TO FIX THE AMERICAN ECONOMY

We create NEW JOBS in all sectors of America's PRIVATE SECTOR. Our economy today is TOO DEPENDENT ON PUBLIC SECTOR JOBS. The two growth industries in America are jobs in health care and education. Both those public sector industries provide jobs with taxpayers' money.

To call a spade a spade, both health care and education ARE SOCIALISTIC. Both will need more and more taxpayers' money in the years to come.

Health care and higher education have become TOO EXPENSIVE for most Americans to pay for by themselves.

DECREASE PUBLIC SECTOR JOBS AND INCREASE PRIVATE SECTOR JOBS

That's the key that WILL JUMP START our economy. Further interest rate cuts WILL NOT HELP.

How did our American economy become (as we are today) SO DEPENDENT on public sector jobs? Or should I rephrase the question and ask WHERE did all our private sector jobs go?

We can blame UNFAIR free world trade (which is controlled by world-wide corporations) for our loss of domestic jobs in our PRIVATE SECTOR.

Most everything we USE or WEAR in America is made in a foreign country.

I guess there was a SHORT TERM advantage of flooding our American market with foreign goods which took away millions of jobs in our private sector.

The short term advantage was that these tons of foreign goods in our American marketplace HELD DOWN INFLATION for the past 10 years. I guess this simplistic reason for inflation is TOO MUCH MONEY chasing TOO FEW GOODS AND SERVICES.

There has been little or no inflation in the American economy for the past 10 years, NOT ONLY because of foreign goods flooding America's marketplace but because the American consumer HAS NOT GOT TOO MUCH MONEY.

I have to LAUGH when I hear over the news media that America's CONSUMER SPENDING (which accounts for 2/3 of our economy) may pull us out of a RECESSION or conversely if CONSUMER CONFIDENCE is down and they don't spend then we will have a PROLONGED RECESSION.

THE TRUTH OF THE MATTER IS

The majority of average American consumers are head over heels in debt. However, the American consumer will KEEP SPENDING as long as credit is EXTENDED to them and they can buy big ticket items with LITTLE or NO down payment.

The majority of American consumers will CONTINUE to BUY NOW and PAY LATER. So CONSUMER SPENDING and CONSUMER CONFIDENCE has little to do with HOW we replace the DEAD BATTERY which has driven our economy to a standstill.

My next week's political column will provide suggestions of how we can return America's free enterprise system BACK TO the PRIVATE SECTOR.

60

MY VIEWS ON ILLEGAL IMMIGRATION

I just read a draft of my book and realized I couldn't write a political book without my opinion on illegal immigration.

A *READER'S DIGEST* **VERSION OF MY VIEWS ON ILLEGAL IMMIGRATION**

My father and mother immigrated to America from the northern part of Italy as children. They went through Ellis Island and were stamped W.O.P., which meant WITHOUT PAPERS. So I guess technically they were illegal. At least they didn't change my father's first name to TONY and ship him to New York.

Seriously, we all know what part immigrants played in building the great United States of America. The problem we have in America today is not with immigration but with illegal immigration. We must secure our own borders with Mexico and Canada, then set up an Ellis Island Building to process illegal immigrants as soon as possible into American citizens who pay all taxes, their own educational costs, and their own health care costs.

Once we secure our borders and start processing new American citizens, we must deal with the 16 to 20 million illegals we have living in America today.

One must remember the majority of hard working, law abiding illegals are assets to the American economy if they become citizens.

I say if they have a steady job for one year they can become naturalized citizens within six months. This way U.S. law enforcement can sort out the newly made U.S. citizens from the illegal criminals.

Of course we will have to raise the minimum wage about $2 per hour and of course the newly made citizens would probably have to work two or three jobs (like the rest of our lower income and middle income Americans).

We must not continue to let big business (National Chamber of Commerce), etc., etc., bring in illegal workers and not pay them a living wage.

Other American citizens are being taxed to subsidize their education, health care, and costs of increased law enforcement.

It's time we American citizens realize being an American citizen isn't the big deal it used to be. Most Americans are poor, lower income, and middle income, are in debt or living from paycheck to paycheck.

America needs hard working, law abiding citizens who want to live the American Dream even if it takes the whole family to do it.

Will my solution to illegal immigration be fair to all? Hell no, but who said life was fair?

www.ingramcontent.com/pod-product-compliance
Lightning Source LLC
Chambersburg PA
CBHW020245290526
45784CB00003B/1110